NÂZIM HİKMET · BEYOND THE WALLS

Nâzım Hikmet

BEYOND THE WALLS

Selected Poems

Translated by
Ruth Christie, Richard McKane,
Talât Sait Halman

Introduced by
Talât Sait Halman

ANVIL PRESS POETRY
in association with
YAPI KREDİ YAYINLARI

Published in 2002
by Anvil Press Poetry Ltd
Neptune House 70 Royal Hill London SE10 8RF
www.anvilpresspoetry.com
in association with Yapı Kredi Yayınları, Istanbul
Reprinted with corrections 2002
Reprinted 2003, 2007

This book is published with financial assistance
from Arts Council England
and Yapı Kredi, Istanbul

Designed and set in Monotype Ehrhardt by Anvil
Printed and bound in England
by Cromwell Press, Trowbridge, Wiltshire

ISBN 0 85646 329 9

CONTENTS

The Epic of the War of Independence

Poems Written Between 9 and 10 at Night (for his wife Piraye)

From Four Prisons

Quatrains

In Bursa's Fortress Prison

New Poems

Last Poems

APPENDIX

Early Poems (1913–1925)

INTRODUCTION

Nâzım Hikmet: Turkey's Romantic Revolutionary

Nâzım Hikmet died in June 1963 at the age of 61. Had he lived another ten, twenty, twenty-five years, he would probably have been awarded the Nobel Prize for Literature. He was and remains his country's best-known modern poet at home and abroad. In 2002 the centennial of his birth will be observed in Turkey and as a UNESCO international year.

A powerful voice against exploitation and injustice, Nâzım Hikmet wrote as a rebel for 40 years and spent nearly two-thirds of his adult life in prison and exile. A confirmed Marxist-Leninist, he expressed his ideological convictions and utopian visions in exquisite lyrics that ran the gamut from invective to sentimentality.

In modern Turkey, which has witnessed cataclysmic changes since 1918, Nâzım Hikmet was the first – and most stirring – voice of iconoclasm. An avowed communist whose views clashed with government policy, he advocated leftist causes in much of his poetry, preaching justice for the disenfranchised and affirming a staunch faith in revolution. In the early Twenties, he introduced free verse and presided over the demise of stanzaic form and stringent prosody. Nâzım Hikmet had a lyric power virtually unequalled by any other modern Turkish poet, and a highly developed faculty for dramatizing the human predicament. Not only his poems of love and exile but also some of his political verses are marked by their moving spirit which, even in translation, comes across with telling effect. Nâzım Hikmet earned international renown through the lyric flow of his statements, as well as the poignancy and optimism of his best work, though detractors claim that he found fame outside Turkey thanks to the literary propaganda efforts of the Soviet Union and other socialist countries where he had lived or visited.

Nâzım Hikmet lived and wrote like a romantic revolutionary during much of his stormy and tragic life which ended in Moscow in 1963. He was a crusading poet who railed against injustice and inertia in Turkey and elsewhere. Because of his ideology he served jail terms totalling almost fifteen years and suffered the suppression of his poetry for nearly half his career. The vicissitudes in the private and public lives of few poets have been as inextricable from their poetry as were Nâzım Hikmet's. Much of his best work is an account of the dramatic events of his life: years of imprisonment, fellow revolutionaries and inmates, exile unto death, heart failures, in an autobiographical vein. But even poems where there are no real-life references have fired the imagination of Turkish readers who have found an additional dimension of pathos and cogency in his lines because they knew the circumstances of deprivation and agony that drove Nâzım Hikmet.

Nâzım, as he is often called by his admirers, was born in 1902, son of Hikmet Bey who served as Director of the Turkish government's Press Office and as Consul General. While attending the Naval Academy in Istanbul, he published his first poems at sixteen. His early work followed the fashionable forms of the day. Using the stanzaic patterns and the simple syllabic metres of traditional Turkish folk poetry, he – like most of his contemporaries – confined his themes to love, speculations about life and death, national pride, natural beauties, and modern mysticism.

In 1920 the young poet, already a celebrity in literary circles, left Istanbul, then under Allied occupation, and went to Anatolia where the Turks, under the aegis of Mustafa Kemal Pasha, were engaged in a national liberation struggle. He served briefly as a teacher, came under the influence of 'Spartacist' radicals and revolutionaries, and hailed the Turkish War of Independence as an anti-imperialist struggle and a class uprising. In 1921 the impressionable Nâzım, who had groped for a faith beyond mysticism and patriotism, went to the Soviet Union where communism, as a doctrine in action, fired his imagination and kindled hope for what he liked to call 'sunny days'. He spent about six years in the Soviet Union, studying at the University of the Workers of the East in Moscow and acquiring a passionate attachment to communism, as well as revolutionary ideas about the norms and functions of poetry. The first poem to come out of this new orientation was 'The Pupils of the Eyes of Hungry People', written after seeing in Moscow a film called 'Hungry People':

Hungry people, lined up, hungry,
Neither man nor woman, neither boy nor girl,
Frail and feeble,
With the twisted arms
Of a writhing tree . . .
They are
The walking limbs
Of those
Barren lands . . .
Hungry people, lined up, hungry
Not two or three,
Not five or ten,
Thirty million,
Our hungry
People . . .

This poem, written in the summer of 1921, marked Nâzım Hikmet's adoption of free verse and ideological poetry. Abruptly, he abandoned the formal lyric and ready-made metres. Free verse with alternations of short and long lines, occasional rhyming, and wide use of alliteration, assonance, and onomatopoeia, a staccato syntax, were to remain the hallmarks of his art and his major influences on modern Turkish poetics.

Nâzım's new aesthetics invited comparison with the work of Vladimir Mayakovsky. Many critics took him to task for having used Mayakovsky as his model. Years later, Nâzım Hikmet disclaimed any knowledge of Russian or familiarity with Mayakovsky at the time he wrote 'The Pupils of the Eyes of Hungry People'. A few years before his death, however, he told Ekber Babayev, a Soviet scholar of Turkish literature, that in 1921 he had seen a Mayakovsky poem and found its form interesting, although he had not read it since he knew no Russian, and that he tried to approximate the form in his 'Hungry People'.

A survey of the possible influences of Mayakovsky's verse has yet to be made. Similarly, the occasional charges that he plagiarized at least one Sergei Yesenin poem are awaiting proof. Those interested in literary debts will do well to observe that Nâzım Hikmet himself acknowledged his early familiarity with French vers libre and described some of his poems in the Twenties as 'futuristic'. His futurist phase yielded several poems glorifying the machine age:

> Our excitement
> is an engine
> which even as it glides on rails
> never loses its steel statue grandeur.
> It is ours:
> the engine is the offshoot
> of our consciousness.

In another poem, Nâzım Hikmet simulated the sounds of machinery in expressing his revolutionary yearning for industrialization:

> Trrrrum,
>   trrrum,
>   trrrrum!
> track ticky tack
> I want to become
>   a machine.
> Out of my brain, flesh and bones springs
>   this urge.

A substantive innovation he introduced was materialism, which stood in sharp contrast to the Islamic mysticism and transcendentalism of centuries of classical Ottoman-Turkish poetry and the idealism so typical of European-oriented verse from the middle of the 19th century. Although Turkey's most forceful modernist failed to extend the implications of his materialistic concepts to their outer limits and confined himself to such polemics as 'Those who oppose us / really oppose / the eternal laws / of the dynamics of matter / and society marching forward', he still made Turkish poetry less abstract than ever before. One of his most significant contributions to Turkish poetics was concretization.

After he returned to Turkey from the Soviet Union in 1924, he spent a period of eight months in Turkey, much of it in hiding. In 1928 he was arrested after a further stay in Russia, on grounds of crossing the Soviet border into Turkey without a passport, and charged with spreading communist propaganda. From this era came the resounding declamatory poems in which he denounced, in angry, satiric, or utopian terms, economic injustice and violations of human dignity. His charismatic personality, his torrential poems, his public readings stirred wide interest, and soon the young poet assumed the posture, even the stature, of a literary hero. He was soon to become too obtrusive and effective a voice to be ignored by the government, whose relations with the Soviet Union were deteriorating, and Nâzım Hikmet was jailed despite his assurance that he was 'only concerned with the literary aspects of Marxism and Communism'.

Following his release, he started collecting his poems, and published books in quick succession: *835 Satır* ('835 Lines') and *Jokond ile Si-Ya-U* ('La Gioconda and Si-A-U') in 1929, *Varan 3* ('The Third One') and *1 + 1 = 1* in 1930, *Sesini Kaybeden Şehir* ('The City That Lost Its Voice') in 1931, *Gece Gelen Telgraf* ('Wire Received at Night') and *Benerci Kendini Niçin Öldürdü?* ('Why Did Benerjee Kill Himself?') in 1932, *Portreler* ('Portraits') and *Taranta-Babu'ya Mektuplar* ('Letters to Taranta-Babu') in 1935, and *Şeyh Bedreddin Destanı* ('The Epic of Sheikh Bedreddin') in 1936.

In his verse, as in such avant-garde plays as *Kafatası* ('The Skull') and *Unutulan Adam* ('The Forgotten Man'), Nâzım Hikmet continued his dual role of artistic iconoclast and social critic. 'I conceive of art', he said in the Thirties, 'as an active institution in society. To me, the artist is the engineer of the human soul' (employing Stalin's formula).

In 1929, in an interview, Nâzım Hikmet offered the following observations: 'New poetry – which is the poetry of the city – has a complex composition and technique. In place of the repetitious sounds of rural life, we now have the vast symphony of the city. . . . The new poet makes no distinction between poetic or prosodic or colloquial languages. He uses an all-embracing, unified language which is not newfangled or artificial, but vibrant, colourful, profound, utterly complex – namely, the language itself.'

As he grew more secure in his role as innovator extraordinary, he placed greater stress on syncretism and a comprehensive approach in the creative process. He claimed that his prosody, which was essentially free verse arranged as jagged lines and run-ons, featured a 'special synthesis of traditional Turkish metres, with both melody and harmony, rhymed and unrhymed, the epigrammatic lines and the whole poem – both the violin and the orchestra, structural unity and motion – dynamic forms and metres attuned to the poetry which must reflect and express reality with its past, present, and future, as well as man in his internal and external world functioning within that reality.'

These statements stood in sharp contrast to the poet's earlier – and sometimes biting – denunciations of nonrevolutionary art. In many poems, he had burlesqued his predecessors and contemporaries, and occasionally launched devastating attacks on them: 'You put your soul on auction like a black slave / and turned your skull into a harlot's room.'

As he matured as an artist, Nâzım Hikmet clung to his communist views on the function of literature. He always assigned to himself the task of voicing the deprivations and aspirations of oppressed classes: 'I am the poet of a particular class in industrial society. I speak of the problems, sufferings, and needs of that class.' His aesthetic preference, by the time he was thirty-seven, evolved from what he liked to call 'active realism' into a 'dynamic synthesis'. He described his modified poetics in an interview in 1937 with a candid self-criticism unprecedented for him: 'Balzac's realism is multifaceted. It expresses reality in all its complexity, with all its elements of past, present, and future, and in terms of motion. I aspire to this type of realism, seeking to apply it to poetry. But I have yet to achieve this aim. In most of my writing, realism is still one-dimensional. As a consequence, many of my pieces have an excessively declamatory propaganda aspect. I now realize this mistake. In my future work, I am resolved to avoid the same error. My views of the world remain unchanged, but my ideas about how these views should be expressed are now radically different.'

A survey of Nâzım Hikmet's poetry published between 1921 and 1937 charts the course of the aesthetic evolution from linear concepts to synthesis. His long poems and epics illustrate this growth: *Jokond ile Si-Ya-U* ('La Gioconda and Si-A-U', 1929), reads like a sophomoric political allegory. With *Benerci Kendini Niçin Öldürdü?* ('Why Did Benerjee Kill Himself?', 1932), Nâzım came to realize that political verse can never succeed without infusions of lyricism, but still failed to overcome his strident and simplistic rhetoric. *Taranta Babu'ya Mektuplar* ('Letters to Taranta-Babu', 1935) has dominant lyricism in its crucial passages, and dramatic dimension, but the prose sections, including news items, deprive the poem of architectural unity and integrity. All three books are bitter denunciations of imperialism, capitalism, and fascism.

The internalization of injustice and oppression in 'Letters to Taranta-Babu' enabled the poet to indict Mussolini's fascism and Ethiopian campaign in far more effective terms than he had been able to use against imperialism and political terror in the earlier books.

Nâzım Hikmet's masterpiece, *Şeyh Bedreddin Destanı* ('The Epic of Sheikh Bedreddin'), came out in 1936. It represents the culmination of the best aspects of the poet's art and it is remarkably free of his weaknesses. The epic is a lyrical and dramatic account of the uprisings of Şeyh Bedreddin and his followers, including a young revolutionary named Börklüce Mustafa, who founded a religious sect advocating community ownership, social and judicial equality, etc., in the early 15th century. Nâzım Hikmet tells how the Ottoman armies, under the command of Royal Prince Murad, crushed the uprisings, killed Börklüce Mustafa, and later hanged Şeyh Bedreddin. This work is a perfect synthesis of substance and form, of diction and drama, of fact and metaphor. Bedreddin and Mustafa are treated as tragic heroes whose ideals are thwarted by a cruel death. Nâzım Hikmet's ideological concerns are, fortunately for the poem, woven into the action and lyric formulation. An elegiac tone, fully attuned to the historical narrative, precludes the intrusion of the polemics and propaganda which have had deleterious effects on Nâzım's other major poems. The epic is perhaps the best long poem written in Turkish in this century.

Turkey's most exciting and controversial poet had been in and out of prisons from 1928 to 1933, where he wrote some of his best lyrics as well as much doggerel. In 1938, at the height of his popularity, he was dragged before a military tribunal and condemned to a 28-year prison term on charges of sedition and subversive activity among military students. Imprisonment, coupled with suppression of his books, silenced publication for nearly a dozen years until his release in 1950. He wrote voluminously in prison, however, including a massive work running close to twenty thousand lines entitled *Memleketimden İnsan Manzaraları* ('Humanscapes from my Land').

In 1950, when Turkey was making its transition to a multiparty regime, a concerted effort by Turkish intellectuals, supported by campaigns abroad, prompted the government to release Nâzım Hikmet. A year later he escaped from Turkey to the Soviet Union – presumably to avoid being drafted into the armed forces despite his advanced age and failing health. His departure led to renewed suppression of his books in Turkey where he was stripped of his citizenship. But, during his years in the Soviet Union and other East European countries (he took Polish citizenship and adopted the surname Borzecki), his international reputation grew. Recipient, with Pablo Neruda, of the 1950 International Peace Price of the Soviet Union, he was featured in *Poèmes de Nazim Hikmet* by Tristan Tzara and Hasan Gureh (Paris, 1951), followed by Ekber Babayev's *Nazym Khikmet* (Moscow, 1952), *Poems by Nazim Hikmet* (Ali Yunus, translator's pseudonym; New York, 1954), *C'est un dur métier que l'exil* (translated by Charles Dobzynsky with the poet's collaboration; Paris, 1957), *In quest' anno 1941* (Milan, 1958) and several other collections in many East European languages. In the fifties Moscow saw productions of Nâzım Hikmet's plays, including *Ferhat ile Şirin* ('Ferhat and Şirin'), the dramatization of a traditional Turkish love legend, and 'Who Is Ivan Ivanovich?', a blistering satire on bureaucracy.

In his native land, Nâzım Hikmet remained a myth in the fifties, as he had been while in prison from 1938 to 1950. The poet said to a friend: 'A ceasefire will start between my country and me after my death.' (In the late sixties, however, when the Turkish Labour Party MP, writer Çetin Altan, referred to Nâzım as 'a great poet' a fist fight broke out on the floor of the parliament. In 2001 the moving of his remains from Moscow to his native land was still a topic of intense debate and the restoration of his Turkish citizenship met with angry resistance from some cabinet members.) He was homesick: his most moving poems written outside Turkey are testaments of exile and longing. In the Bulgarian town of Varna, he wrote woeful lines: 'To the

Bosphorus a ship starts its trip/Nâzım gently strokes the ship/And his hands burn.' There is so far no documentary evidence to show whether Nâzım Hikmet was favourably impressed by Soviet communism or East European socialism in action, but his poems testify to his nostalgia and lead one to assume that nationalist sentiments outweighed his convictions about world communism.

Prison and exile, while checking his bravura, gave Nâzım Hikmet's verse a dimension of pathos, secret tears, a central drama. His political poems, particularly those published since his escape to the Soviet Union, are vacuous and raucous, but his exile poems ring true. One of his early critics, Peyami Safa, had observed that 'contrary to all his claims to materialism, Nâzım Hikmet is an intensely romantic, lyric, mushy, sentimental poet.' The troubles of later years removed his tendency to melodrama, enabling him to concentrate on stark realities and essential emotions.

Death came to Nâzım Hikmet in June 1963 in Moscow. The 'ceasefire' he had predicted for Turkey and himself actually started shortly after his death. Turkish publishers raced to make available to the Turkish public as much of his unpublished poetry as they could find. Among the major books which came out after 1963 are *Saat 21–22 Şiirleri* ('Poems Written Between 9 and 10 at Night'), *Rubailer* ('Quatrains'), *Dört Hapisaneden* ('From Four Prisons'), and the five-volume *Memleketimden İnsan Manzaraları* ('Humanscapes from my Land').

Rubailer features Nâzım Hikmet's quatrains in which, according to a letter he wrote to his wife in 1945, he tries to revolutionize a time-honoured literary form: 'Taking strength from your love, I shall do something that has never been done in Oriental or Western literatures: I shall attempt to express materialism in rubaiyat.' The attempt seems to have failed, because the themes of materialism are seldom evident in this collection, and the four-line poems cannot even be considered as *rubaiyat* in the real sense of the literary term. But many individual quatrains in the book are among his best short lyrics.

Memleketimden İnsan Manzaraları is a sprawling, episodic saga of the 20th century ranging in theme from the decadence of Turkish aristocrats to World War II. It was designed by the poet as his magnum opus, and is characterized by many critics as a masterpiece, although there have been a few dissenting voices that consider it 'a failure on a grand scale'. After death Nâzım's fame spread further outside of Turkey. New translations of his poems were published in Germany, France, Soviet Union, East Europe, England and USA. In England Taner Baybars and Richard McKane published excellent translations. In the United States, Mutlu Konuk and Randy Blasing produced no fewer than ten volumes of Nâzım's selected poems as well as a full translation of *Memleketimden İnsan Manzaraları*. In 1999 a full-fledged biography by Saime Göksu and Edward Timms (with a preface by Yevgeny Yevtushenko) came out in England under the title of *Romantic Communist: The Life and Work of Nazım Hikmet*.

At a commemorative service held in Paris in December 1964, Tristan Tzara said of him: 'The life Nâzım led engulfs the experiences of a large segment of mankind. His poetry exalts the aspirations of the Turkish people as well as articulating the common ideals of all nations in humanistic terms.' Jean-Paul Sartre sent a message to the Paris ceremony: 'I should like to pay tribute to his great human qualities and his indomitable energy. I met him when he was desperately ill and I was astonished at his determination to live and fight. Unlike others, this man who had endured torment and escaped death would never rest. For him, nothing ever came to an end . . . He knew that man is something to be made – and he has yet to be made – and that man must create himself by a ceaseless fight against the foe.'

Although Turkish officialdom had come to terms with Nâzım Hikmet's stature at home and abroad – Turkish Presidents sometimes quote his poems in their formal speeches, cabinet members and mayors pay visits to his tomb in Moscow, and the Ministry of Culture organizes memorial programmes – controversy still raged at the beginning of the 21st century. Political circles debate the issue of transferring Hikmet's remains from Moscow to Turkey. By 2001 more than half a million signatures were collected in support of a petition asking for the restoration of his citizenship which had been abrogated in 1950.

The literary career of Nâzım Hikmet, spanning four and a half decades from 1918 to 1963, illustrates the vital problems of the poetry of engagement. In poem after poem, where Nâzım mouths sheer invective or ideological polemics, or tries to communicate in prosy statements, banality sets in and curtails the effectiveness of both aesthetic appeal and doctrinal substance. But in those poems which communalize the poet's private self in dynamic terms or internalize communal experiences in lyric formulations, even the political content gains a cogency beyond the validity of its concepts. Nâzım Hikmet's best political poems are, in fact, those which are most lyrical. He achieved success when he used doctrine not as theme or argument but as unspecified context.

At his best, he has been compared by Turkish and non-Turkish men of letters to such figures as Lorca, Aragon, Mayakovsky, Yesenin, Neruda, Artaud, et al. To be sure, his work bears resemblances to these poets and owes them occasional debts of form and stylistic device, but Nâzım Hikmet's literary personality is unique in terms of the synthesis he made of iconoclasm and lyricism, of ideology and poetic diction.

TALÂT SAİT HALMAN
Ankara, 2001

GUIDE TO TURKISH PRONUNCIATION

â   long *a* as in *psalm*

c   as *j* in *judge*

ç   as *ch* in *chapel*

ğ   silent, but lengthens preceding vowels: *Uludağ* is
     pronounced 'Uludah'

ı   as *a* in *along*. It is capitalized as 'I', while a stan-
     dard, dotted *i* has its dot capitalized.

ö   as German *ö* in *Köln* or French *œ* in *œuf*

ş   as *sh* in *lash*

ü   as French *u* in *tu*

TRANSLATORS' PREFACE

I

Nâzım Hikmet's name first came my way in 1949, in a slim grey book of translations entitled *The Star and the Crescent*, an anthology of modern Turkish poetry selected by Derek Patmore and published in 1946 by Constable & Co. I remember being puzzled by the editor's reference to 'one of the best of the younger contemporary poets' whose poems were not included in his selection, 'for reasons beyond my control'. What were these reasons?

I was to learn the answer to the question many years later when I became involved in the study of Turkish language and literature at SOAS, where Professor Ménage and Dr Bainbridge guided us with humour, wit and erudition through the original Turkish of many poets, old and modern. Dr Bainbridge, in particular, fired us with enthusiasm for Nâzım Hikmet's love poems to his wife from prison which Richard McKane was to translate with warmth and simplicity.

Although Nâzım Hikmet is recognized as a major international poet and has been widely translated into many languages including English, in this country he is little known, for reasons we can only guess. English translations published here from the work of this prolific writer are not substantial in content. The earliest are two short selections by Taner Baybars in 1967 and 1972, and those by Nermin Menemencioğlu and others in her 1978 *Penguin Book of Turkish Verse*; the Greville Press published a small selection of translations by Taner Baybars and Richard McKane in 1990. Feyyaz Kayacan Fergar's *Modern Turkish Poetry* (published in 1992 by the Rockingham Press) also includes several translations. In 1999 the comprehensive detailed biography of Nâzım Hikmet by Saime Göksu and Edward Timms includes several translations by themselves and others. No larger collection has appeared in this country. The translations of Mutlu Konuk and Randy Blasing, published in America, are not to be found in bookshops here. We saw a need for English readers to have greater access to certain elements of Nâzım Hikmet's work and we hope that our selection will go some way to remedy the lack.

At present there is no edition of Hikmet's work with commentary. However it is to be hoped that a forthcoming Yapı Kredi edition will incorporate full notes to the poems.

We have included in an appendix translations of seven early poems dating from Nâzım Hikmet's teens and not published in his lifetime. They seem to us to demonstrate the difference between poems which conformed to the metrical and lyrical conventions of a previous age, and the revolutionary changes that began in his work when he first went to Moscow in 1921 and came under Mayakovsky's influence. He brought politics and its language into his work, merging lyrical and satirical styles and this continued all his life.

At the same time we find it of interest that many of his youthful concerns were to persist through a lifetime of writing: his love for the landscapes of his country; his compassion for the underdog; his anger at injustice and religious fanaticism; his optimism and conviction that one day humanity will be 'free of the circle'; and not least, his love of women.

We are grateful to Yapı Kredi Yayınları in Turkey for their support in aiding us to complete this project, and to our many Turkish friends who were at the end of the line at the right time to suggest or confirm 'le mot juste'. It was a suggestion from Feyyaz Kayacan Fergar (who translated the beautiful last poem in this selection, 'My Funeral') that set me to work on my first translation of Nâzım Hikmet, 'Extracts from the Diary of La Gioconda'. I will always remember Feyyaz Fergar with affection and gratitude for his encouragement and enthusiasm. Moris Farhi and Stephen Watts gave generously of their time and attention. But my greatest personal debt is to the Turkish novelist Vedat Türkali. To his lifelong regret, as a young man teaching in the Army, he was obliged to conceal his own communist sympathies and had failed to meet the poet on any of the few occasions Hikmet was released from prison. Then and later the poet became an ikon for the novelist, of courage, idealism, fortitude and hope. My friend Bridget Lewer and I were privileged to visit him frequently in his London flat where we heard his views on Nâzım Hikmet as a man and a poet. In Türkali's eyes the two were inseparable. Vedat was a mine of information on Nâzım, always ready to share it generously with us, making sure 'we got it right'. The pride of his life is an embroidered white shirt that had belonged to Nâzım Hikmet, had been given to Vedat by a mutual friend of Hikmet and Türkali and which Vedat now wears on special festive occasions only – like achieving the conclusion of a novel. As though he dedicates each novel to the memory of his hero.

Last but not least, my part of the project owes everything to the computer skills of my husband James, who worked patiently and untiringly to transcribe the manuscripts into a PC-friendly form. I would also like to thank the editors of *Modern Turkish Poetry*, *Southfields* and *Acumen* where some of my translations have appeared.

RUTH CHRISTIE

2

On my first visit to Turkey in 1966 I found myself in a bookshop in Istanbul, asking in my rudimentary Turkish for some Turkish poetry. The book I went away with was the recently published first volume of Nâzım Hikmet's *Human Landscapes* in Turkish. On further trips to Turkey I managed to come to grips with the language, but it was still easier for me to read Nâzım Hikmet in Russian in 1971 in the British Museum Oriental Reading Room. About that time Taner Baybars' slim Cape volume of Hikmet came out, to be followed by his *Moscow Symphony* and a Carcanet volume *The Day After Tomorrow*. In the early 1970s I met Nermin Menemencioğlu, one of the first translators into English of Nâzım Hikmet, who had known him personally. She had started work on her *Penguin Book of Turkish Verse* which, though long out of print, remains a benchmark of Turkish poetry, and in which some of my early translations of Hikmet were printed. The best known translations, by Randy Blasing and Mutlu Konuk, have not been published in the UK, but were published in the States by Persea Books from the 1970s onwards.

In the 1970s, when I lived in Turkey for some years, I bought my favourite collections of Hikmet: *From Four Prisons* and *Poems Written Between 9* and *10 at Night* (for his wife Piraye). At that time the 'dark brown voice' of Ruhi Su for me resonated with the true spirit of Nâzım Hikmet. My copy of *The War of Independence* was burnt by an apprehensive friend when I left it with him when I returned to England for a few months. In those years Nâzım Hikmet, who had been subject to censorship in Turkey and remained a dangerous poet to have on one's bookshelf, became well published in Turkey by Bilgi Yayınevi, Cem Yayınevi (this edition had some notes) and finally in the 1980s by Adam: the 8 volumes of poetry which Ruth Christie and I used as our texts, selecting poems from each volume except the long poem *Human Landscapes*, from which we were loath to excerpt. In 1990 Greville Press published a Hikmet pamphlet *A Sad State of Freedom* translated by Taner Baybars and myself, where I contributed some of the 'Poems to Piraye'.

I would like to acknowledge the late Abidin Dino, artist and illustrator of Nâzım Hikmet, who talked to me in Paris about Nâzım Hikmet's writing method of composing as he paced up and down as in a cell – known in Turkish as 'volta' – and of his love of the radio. I would also like to acknowledge Hakkı Gökmen and Altan Koraltan (for his setting up and distribution of a xeroxed pamphlet of mine, *Nazım Hikmet Prison Poems* in the 1980s) for help on very early versions of 'Flaxen Hair' and 'A Cracked Washbasin' respectively.

Conversations with Nâzım's Russian friends Andrei Voznesensky and Rady Fish were stimulating, and the latter's Russian edition of Hikmet's poems was, just occasionally, a useful source of the odd word – for both Ruth Christie and I had applied a golden rule of translation, of not reading the precursor translations while we were translating. Readers of Hikmet owe a great debt to the first biography in English of Nâzım Hikmet by Saime Göksu and Edward Timms, entitled *Romantic Communist: The Life and Work of Nazım Hikmet* (Hurst).

We would like to thank Professor Talât Sait Halman for his support of the project, his translations and his introduction. Moris Farhi, former chair of International PEN Writers in Prison Committee gave generously of his insights into Hikmet. The late Feyyaz Kayacan Fergar, the inspirational poet, prose writer and translator, published several of our translations of Hikmet in his anthology *Modern Turkish Poetry* (Rockingham Press). Not so long before his own death he translated the Hikmet poem 'My Funeral' which to all intents and purposes closes the book, though we decided to include an appendix of Hikmet's early poems.

We would like to thank Yapı Kredi Yayınları, and Selçuk Altun and Güven Turan in particular, for their sponsorship and co-publication of this book. We would also like to thank Peter Jay of Anvil Press for his belief in the project.

Finally I'd like to thank Ruth Christie for all the long friendly hours of translation we put in together with the computing and editorial support of her husband James. It became a true collaboration – as it had been with *Voices of Memory: Selected Poems of Oktay Rifat* (Rockingham Press) – and as we climbed the steep mountains of Nâzım Hikmet's poetry we took it in turns to 'lead'.

As we approach Nâzım Hikmet's 100th anniversary in January 2002, I still find his optimism is exhilarating and goes so much deeper than belief in 'the bright future'. At the same time, to paraphrase Anna Akhmatova, he 'located the blackest wound / but somehow couldn't heal it.' For thousands and thousands of Turkish speakers Nâzım Hikmet is a symbol of resistance, a rallying point, yet he is also capable of expressing their most intimate feelings. It has been an honour to translate his poems, to interpret his feelings, to tussle with his ideas and language.

Some of these translations have appeared in earlier versions in *The Penguin Book of Turkish Verse* (1978), *Nazim Hikmet: A Sad State of Freedom* (Greville Press, 1990), *Modern Turkish Poetry* (Rockingham, 1992), *Voices of Conscience* (Iron Press, 1995), *Poet for Poet* (Hearing Eye, 1998), *Southfields* and the Turkish PEN magazine. My thanks to their editors.

I dedicate my share of this book to my daughter Juliet who loves Nâzım Hikmet's poetry and read it with me on a reading trip to America in 1998.

RICHARD MCKANE
London, September 2000

WEEPING WILLOW

The water flowed,
it showed
willow trees in its mirror,
weeping willows washing their hair in the stream.
Red riders raced towards the sinking sun,
their flaming swords drawn to strike the willows.
Suddenly
like a bird
    shot
      in the wing
a wounded horseman tumbled from his horse.
He did not shout,
or call after those who passed,
he just looked with brimming eyes
    at the flashing hooves of the riders receding.

Alas!
    alas that he
will never lie again on the foaming necks of his galloping
    horses,
or brandish his sword chasing after the white armies!

Gradually hoofbeats die away,
the riders are lost in the sunset.

Horsemen, horsemen, red riders,
horses   wind   winged
horses   wind   wing . . .
horses   wind . . .
horses . . .
horse . . .

Life passed like the wind winged horsemen.

The sound of the running water stopped.
Shadows grew denser
colours were wiped away.
Black blinds came down,
on his blue eyes,
the weeping willows leant
over his fair hair.

Don't weep weeping willow,
don't weep,
in the dark mirror of water, don't fold your hands,
don't fold your hands,
don't weep.

1928

THE WORM IN MY BODY

Like a soft
white worm
you entered
my body which is a pine tree
as tall as a minaret
and you gnawed at me!
I carry you inside me
the way a British worker
carries in his intestines
that worm, Macdonald!

I know
        who's to blame!

Oh, woman, whose soul
        is the House of Lords!
You, hairless Poincaré wearing a long dress!
The simplest ploy of yours
is to burn
        in front of me
like an engine whose furnace
        makes the iron bars red hot.
Another simple trick of yours is
to weave in and out
        like skates on ice.
Cold!
Hot!
You slut,
stop!
With your soft
        white
           wriggling
you're entering my brain
        and gnawing at it!

You can't go into my brain,
you can't gnaw at my brain!

Like a rotten tooth
   I pulled out the worm
that had crept into my brain
with those soft
      white wrigglings.
It took a lot of toil and sweat!
This will be the last!
              Never again!

1924

TO BECOME A MACHINE

I live in a four-storey wooden house,
my room's on the fourth floor.
Across from my window
is a twenty-storey reinforced-concrete block of flats.
Twenty lifts work every moment
from roof to basement,
from basement to roof.
But I –
a man who wants to set an engine in his belly
and fix a couple of screws to his tail –
every evening
climb eighty steps of a wooden stairway.
At every step my resentment increases a hundredfold
against the tenants who go up by lift.
But I'm still optimistic.
I believed . . .
machines would be ours
and that I would become a machine.
Only till then,
to soothe my great desire,
every morning
I launch myself from the fourth floor
down the banisters of eighty steps
vizzz . . .
I slide . . .
The old woman porter says
'Crazy!' to me,
not knowing that I – what an idiot!
want
to become a machine . . .

16 *January* 1923
Moscow

EXTRACTS FROM THE DIARY OF LA GIOCONDA

Paris, 15 March, 1924
The Louvre

I'm bored in the Louvre these days.
One soon grows tired of boredom.
So now I'm bored with my boredom.
From this spiritual *crise*
    I formed the opinion:
    It's fun
        to explore the Museum,
        but not to be one of its treasures!

Condemned to this palace, prison of the past,
            sentenced to grin without end,
under the oil paint my face is beginning
            to crack with ennui
because
    I was La Gioconda of Florence,
my smile better-known than my city.

I'm bored in the Louvre these days.
and since it soon gets boring talking with the past,
I
    decided from now on
to keep a diary.
Perhaps writing up this day
    will help to forget the last.

The Louvre is a funny place.
Here you can find:
Alexander the Great's
            chronometric Longines watch.
But
    you can't find a common pencil
or a sheet of clean paper to write on.

Damn your Paris, your Louvre!
I'll write my memoirs
  on the back of my portrait.

Look here:
I've made a beginning
by stealing a fountain-pen
  from a short-sighted American
who sticks his red nose in my skirts,
his hair reeking of wine!
I'm writing on the back of my picture
the agony of one whose smile is famous!

March 18. Night

The Louvre asleep.
In the gloom the armless Venus
  resembles a world war soldier.
A Chevalier's golden helmet gleams:
the nightwatch torches light on
  an obscure painting.
Here
in the Louvre
every day is the same as another
  like the sides of a wooden cube.
My head filled with pungent smells
  like a shelf in a chemist's shop.

March 20

I admire the Flemish painters.
Was it easy to give the look of a naked goddess
to the plump mistress of a sausage-merchant?
Though
  she could buy silk knickers if she liked
a cow + silken knickers is still a cow!

Last night
        a window
                was left open.
The naked Flemish goddesses caught cold.
Today
all day
        they coughed and sneezed
and turned their mountainous pink buttocks
                to the crowds.
I too caught cold.
I sniffed in secret from the visitors,
afraid I'd be a laughing-stock
                with my catarrhal smile.

April 1

Today I saw a Chinese man.
        Not at all in the pigtailed style of old!
And how he looked
        at me!
I know very well the Chinese
exquisite carvers of ivory,
        don't look twice
at a stranger.

April 20

The papers are full of Chinese news.
I hear that now
        the dragon from Kaf,
                the mountain surrounding the world,
                        has spread its wings
in the golden firmament
over the Chinese homeland.

But as a result
    the throat of a British lord
        shaven like a plucked hen
will be cut,
together with
the long
wispy
beard
of Confucius.

April 22

Last night a screeching American *zurna*,
the horn of a 12-horse Ford
    woke me from a dream.
The moment I saw it
    it vanished.

What I saw was a still blue lake!
In which the slant-eyed love of my life
had embraced a gleaming fish by the neck.
I'm going to him there,
my boat a Chinese saucer,
my sail
    a Japanese sunshade
    of bamboo
    and embroidered in silk.

May 2

Today my Chinaman didn't come.

May 5

Nor today.

May 8

My days are like
            the waiting-room
                        of a station,
    my eyes never off the tracks.

May 10

Greek sculptors!
Miniature painters of Selçuk times!
Weavers of carpets of fire for Cemşid!
Readers of poetry to desert dromedaries!
Dancers like the wind!
Cutters of multifaceted diamonds!
And you
        Maestro Michelangelo!
with your five skills at your fingertips
proclaiming to friend and foe:
La Gioconda's beloved,
for shouting in Paris too loudly
    and smashing the window
        of the CHINESE
                AMBASSADOR
has been evicted
        from France!

My Chinese lover has gone back to China!
I wonder who they'll call
        Leylâ and Mejnun now?

May 13

Today right before me
      a young girl
            was freshening up the lipstick
                  of her blood-red mouth.
As my eye was caught in her mirror,
the tin crown of fame on my head fell to bits.
While the urge to cry twisted my guts
      and distorted my lips,
my face grinned inanely like a roasted pig's.

If I had my way
a cubist painter could take the bones
of that Leonardo da Vinci
and make them into handles for his brushes;
for touching me with his paint-stained hands,
and sticking this cursèd smile
like a gold crown in my mouth,
– it would serve him right!

1929

BAREFOOT

Sun on our head
    a fiery
        turban.
The arid soil
    is sandal to our naked feet.
Beside us
    a villager
        more dead than his ancient mule;
what burns
    is not beside us
        but in our veins.
No shepherd's jacket on our back,
no wrist with a whip to crack,
no horse, no cart,
no gendarme;
bear-den villages,
    mudbuilt towns,
        we climbed the bald hills.
So we wandered in that land!
In the rheumy eyes
    of sick bullocks,
we heard the cry of stony fields.
We saw that now
    the soil no longer gives
        its golden-corn breath
        to the old wooden
        ploughs!
We did not sleepwalk.
    No,
we went from one garbage heap to another.
So we wandered in that land!

We
know
    that country
        and its longings.

A longing
as clearly defined
as a materialist's mind;
in this longing
    there is substance,
       real substance!

1922

THE PROVOCATEUR

This man
    sold his comrade;
On a tray of gold
    this man sold
    the bloody severed head
      of his comrade.

Fear
    prowls in the feet of this man
        like his shadow.
This man
    lives like dark waters.
Every evening when the sun goes down,
he is the one who sneaks up on you
      tiptoeing slowly
dragging his wife's panties on the sidewalk.

You ought to know him
    by the tinkling of the leper's bell
        hanging from his heart,
and you ought to know
    that bit by bit his leprosy
        makes his soul's flesh fall off.

This man is hungry today.
He is hungry,
but in this man
even the great, mighty hunger has lost its sanctity.

This man, friends,
at dusk one day
    sold his comrade;
on a tray of gold
    this man sold
    the bloody severed head
      of his comrade.

1929

MAYBE I

Maybe I
    long before
        that day
    shall sway
    early one morning at the bridgehead
        where I shall thrust my shadow on the asphalt way.

Maybe I
    long after
        that day
– on my shaven cheek my stubble turning grey –
        shall remain alive.

And I
    long after
        that day
        (if I've been able to survive)
shall lean on the side walls of the city squares
    on the evening of a holiday
        and play
the violin to the old-timers
    who survived like myself the last fight.

All around us are the glittering sidewalks
        of a marvellous night
and the steps
    of brave new human beings
        singing brave new songs.

1930

FOUR MEN AND FOUR BOTTLES

A round table.
Four bottles.
Four men
  and four glasses of wine.
It's Médoc.
Wine in the glass
  then none
  then wine again.
Four men drinking wine . . .

One empty bottle.
One of them said:
'Tomorrow I'll play it brilliantly,
  it'll all be over after my first word;
    he'll definitely hang . . .'

Three empty bottles.
Three men answered,
three mouths answered:
'We'll definitely hang him.'

A round table,
four empty bottles
  and four men . . .

1930

ADVICE TO OUR CHILDREN

You're allowed to be naughty,
to scramble up steep walls
            and climb high trees.
Let your captain's skill steer your bicycle
            as it speeds away
                    like lightning.
With your lead-pencil that draws funny pictures
of your Religious Knowledge professor,
destroy that green-turbaned skeleton
            of Holy Scriptures.
Build your own paradise
            on the black earth;
and whoever spins you the yarn of 'Adam's Creation',
            take a geography book and refute them.
Acknowledge only this earth,
            believe in this earth.
Don't distinguish between your own mother
                    and mother earth.
Love the earth
        as you love your mother . . .

1928

THE BLUE-EYED GIANT, THE MINIATURE WOMAN AND THE HONEYSUCKLE

He was a blue-eyed giant,
he loved a miniature woman.
The woman's dream was of a miniature house
   with a garden where honeysuckle grows
     in a riot of colours
      that sort of house.

The giant loved like a giant,
and his hands were used to such big things
   that the giant could not
make the building,
   could not knock on the door
of the garden where the honeysuckle grows
     in a riot of colours
      at that house.

He was a blue-eyed giant,
he loved a miniature woman,
a mini miniature woman.
The woman was hungry for comfort
   and tired of the giant's long strides.
And bye bye off she went to the embraces of a rich dwarf
   with a garden where the honeysuckle grows
     in a riot of colours
      that sort of house.

Now the blue-eyed giant realizes,
there can't even be a grave for giant loves:
in the garden where honeysuckle grows
     in a riot of colours
      that sort of house . . .

BEFORE HE LEFT

Over the window-panes night and snow.
Railtracks gleaming snow-white in the dark –
reminding us we could be carried away and never brought back.
A barefoot youth
         head wrapped in black
lies in the third-class waiting room
            of the station.
                I walk up and down . . .

Night and snow at the windows.
Inside they're singing a song.
My brother's favourite song before he left
His best-loved song . . .
His best-loved . . .
His best . . . . . .

Friends, don't look at my eyes
I'm near to tears . . .

Railtracks gleaming snow-white in the dark –
reminding us we could be carried away and never brought back.
A barefoot youth
         head wrapped in black
lies in the third-class waiting room
            of the station . . .

Night and snow at the windows.
Inside they're singing a song! . . .

1933

THREE CYPRESSES

Three cypresses stood in front of my doorway.
Three cypresses.
In the wind, those cypresses used to sway.
Three cypresses.
Heads soaring to the stars from roots in the ground
three cypresses.
They swayed, those cypresses, in the wind.
Three cypresses.
One night my house was raided by my enemies.
Three cypresses.
Lying in my bed, I was killed.
Three cypresses.
From their roots, those cypresses were felled.
Three cypresses.
No longer heads in the stars, roots in the ground
three cypresses.
They no longer sway, those cypresses, in the wind.
Three cypresses.
Chopped up, there in the marble fireplace, they lie,
three cypresses.
A bloody hatchet is lit up by
three cypresses.

MY POETRY

I don't have a mount with a saddle worked in silver,
I've no private means,
no property, no land.
All I own is a pot of honey.
Its colour redder than fire,
                    a pot of honey!

My honey is all I have . . .
I keep my property and land,
my pot of honey, I mean –
safe from vermin.
But wait, friend, wait . . .
While I have honey in my pot
the bees will come
                    from as far away as Baghdad . . .

1935

TO BE BLIND

[*From the sixth letter to Taranta-Babu*]

How good it is to be blind,
how good to love darkness.
No light like a flashing sword
nor the weight of colours
nor swarming shapes . .
How good it is to love darkness . .

How good it is to be blind.
Your shuttered eyes
        turned inwards,
sitting on the shore you'll watch
the waves of your inner sea.
Your shuttered eyes turned inwards . .

How good it is to be blind.
It is only the blind
        who remain alone with their hearts.
Their eyes give us nothing
from our eyes they get nothing.
It is only the blind
        who remain alone with their hearts.

How good it is to love darkness.
darkness is like God and stands apart.
Darkness is like death
        it has no colour
          no harmony
            darkness has no peer.

Blind ones, prophets of darkness,
scatter the crowd around you with your sticks.
How good it is to be blind,
how good to love darkness.

EIGHTH LETTER TO TARANTA-BABU

Mussolini talks too much, Taranta-Babu!
By himself
    all alone
        like a child abandoned
            in the dark
                screaming
awakening himself with his shriek
kindled with fear
        burning up with fear
he talks without a pause.
Mussolini talks too much, Taranta-Babu.
Because he's terribly scared
        he talks terribly long!

THE EPIC OF SHEIKH BEDREDDİN

In 1933 Hikmet was arrested, tried and sent to Bursa prison.

Late one night in the prison, Nâzım was reading a contemptuous account, recently published, by an Islamic professor of theology, of a fifteenth-century socialist peasant uprising in Western Anatolia. The leader of the revolt, Bedreddin, son of the Kadı of Simavne, was a scholar, a judge and a Sheikh, who had radical ideas in a feudal age. He advocated the sharing of property and the abolition of laws that discriminated against religious minorities.

In 1417, his disciple Mustafa Börklüce began a subversive movement which gathered momentum and included in its following Anatolian peasants, Greeks and Jews. Three years later it was crushed by the Sultan. Mustafa was tortured, nailed to a cross and torn to pieces, his disciples executed: Bedreddin was tried and hanged and four thousand of his followers killed.

Deeply moved as he followed the ideals and heroic struggles of this early socialist revolt, Nâzım fell into a half-dreamlike trance, compounded by a migraine; he imagined he saw one of Mustafa's followers at the window, who guided him on a journey back to the fifteenth century and led him through the sequence of events that led to the defeat and deaths of Mustafa, Bedreddin, and their disciples. Now Nâzım as narrator relates the dream.

I have omitted Nâzım's opening pages, summarized above, which will mean more to Turkish readers than to others. A row of dots indicates a few other similar but much shorter omissions.

[TRANSLATOR'S NOTE]

The Dream

I had a splitting headache. I looked at my watch. It had stopped. The rattle of chains above us had quietened a little and only one of the prisoners was walking up and down. Probably the one sitting alone at the window on the left.

My heart felt a great longing to hear an Anatolian folksong. And I thought that now if the condemned bandits were to begin singing the song of the mountain pastures again from their ward my headache would immediately clear up.

Lighting another cigarette, I bent down and picked up Mehemmed Şerefedin's treatise from the cement floor. Outside the wind was rising, the sea under our window was muttering, and drowning the sounds of chains and whistles. Beneath our

51

window would be rocky cliffs. So often we had wished to look at the point where our wall and the sea met but it was impossible. The iron bars of the window were so close, a man couldn't put his head out. And here we could only see the sea as the horizon. Şefik the turner's bed was next to mine. Şefik murmured something in his sleep and rolled over. The bridal quilt his wife had sent slipped off. I covered him up.

I opened again at the sixty-fifth page of the Professor of Islamic Studies from the Theology Faculty. . . I had just read a few lines from the Sultan's private secretary to the Genoese when through my headache I heard a voice saying:

'Silently I crossed the sea and now I am beside you.'

I turned round. There was someone behind the window overlooking the sea. He was the one who spoke.

'Have you forgotten what Ducas, the Sultan's private secretary to the Genoese, wrote? Don't you remember he spoke of a Cretan monk who lived in the monastery of Turlut on the island of Chios? Did I not come to this Cretan monk as I come to you now? I, one of Börklüce Mustafa's "dervishes" crossing the sea on naked feet, my head bare, and wrapped in a seamless robe.'

I looked at the speaker of these words. With no possibility at all of holding on anywhere he stood there outside the window-bars at full height. He was just as he described. His seamless robe was white.

Now, writing these lines years later, I think of the Professor from the Theology Faculty. I don't know if Şereffedin is alive or dead but if he's alive and reads what I have written here he will certainly say:

'What a hypocrite! He asserts he is a materialist, but at the same time he claims that, like the Cretan monk, he spoke with Börklüce's disciple who silently crossed the seas centuries ago.'

I seem to hear the great Theology Expert's burst of divine laughter that followed.

But no matter – let His Eminence carry on laughing. Let me tell my adventure.

My headache suddenly cleared. I got up from my bed and walked straight to the window. He took me by the hand and we left the other twenty-eight men asleep in the ward of sweating cement. And suddenly I found myself above the rocks where the

sea and our wall met and which we could never see. Silently
crossing the dark sea-waves side by side with Börklüce's disciple,
I went with him right back beyond the years, centuries back, to
the time of Sultan Giyaseddin Ebülfeth Mehemmed bin ibni
Yezidülkirişçi, or quite simply Çelebi Sultan Mehmed.
And so this journey is the adventure I want to tell you about. I
will try to set down what I saw on the journey, the sounds, the
colours, the actions, the various landscapes, bit by bit, and much
of it – an old habit – in a kind of verse of long and short lines with
occasional rhymes. Like –

I

On the divan a red and green forest of Bursa silk,
on the wall a blue garden of Kütahiya tiles;
wine in silver ewers,
lambs roasted to perfection, in copper dishes.
Çelebi Sultan Mehmet strangled his own brother Musa with
     a bowstring,
washed himself ritual clean with his brother's blood in a
     golden bowl
and ascended the throne as Sultan.
Çelebi was Sultan, but
blowing through Red Osman's land
was a wind,
a scream of sterility, a dirge of death.
The peasant's blinding labour, the sweat of his brow,
was his only fief.
Water-pitchers lay broken and empty
and the cavalry twirled their moustaches by the wells.
The traveller heard on the roads the desperate cry of people
     without land,
the cry of a land without people.
At the journey's end as swords clashed at the castle-gate,
     and foaming horses whinnied,
in the marketplace the merchant guilds were in disarray
     defeated of hope by their Masters.
In short – there was a Sultan, a fief, a wind,
                              a bitter lament.

2

This lake is İznik lake,
still,
dark,
deep,
like well-water
               in the heart of the mountains.

Our lakes here
are misty.
The flesh of their fish is tasteless,
malaria rises from the reed-beds
and the lake people die
               before their beards turn white.

This lake is İznik lake,
beside it lies İznik town.
In İznik town
the blacksmith's anvil is like a broken heart.
Children are hungry.
Women's breasts are like dried fish
and the young men sing no songs.

This town is İznik town.
This house is in the artisan quarter.
In this house
is an old man called Bedreddin.
Short,
       his beard bushy
             and white,
his child's eyes slanting and wily
and his yellow fingers like reeds.

Bedreddin
seated
on a white sheepskin rug,
is writing his 'Teshil'
               in Arabic script.

Kneeling before him
they stare
as at a mountain opposite.
Tall thin Mustafa from Börklüce
with his shaven head
and shaggy eyebrows
stares,
and Torlak Kemal with his eagle's beak . . .
They never tire of staring,
never have their fill
of staring at Bedreddin, exile in İznik.

3
A barefoot woman weeps on the shore.
On the lake a fisherman's empty boat,
                its rope snapped
                floats on the water
                        like a dead bird.
It drifts where the water takes it,
it drifts to the opposite shores to be smashed on the cliffs.

It was evening on İznik lake.
The deep-voiced cavalry of the mountain-tops
have beheaded the sun
                and spilled its blood in the lake.

A barefoot woman weeps on the shore,
her fisherman is chained in the castle
on account of a carp.

It was evening on İznik lake.
Bedreddin bent to the water,
                scooped up a handful and stood.

As the water
dripping through his fingers
returned to the lake,
                he said to himself:

'That fire in my heart
has been kindled
and increases day by day.
Were my heart made of beaten iron
it could not stand the heat
but would melt . . .
Now is the time to appear and start my rebellion!
Now we men of the land go to conquer the land.
When the strength of knowledge, the mystic unity
becomes a reality
we will annul the laws of nations and sects . . .'

*

Next day
the boat breaks up on the lake
        a head is cut off in the castle
                a woman weeps on the shore.
And while the man from Simavne
was writing his 'Teshil',
Torlak Kemal and Mustafa
kissed
        their sheikh's hand.
They tightened the girths of their bay horses
and rode out from İznik gate
a bare sword at their knees
a manuscript in their saddle-bags.

The name of their book was
                'Varidât'.

4

. . . . . .

We heard that Mustafa went forth
at Karaburun in the land of Aydın.
He quoted Bedreddin's words
to the villagers.

We heard: 'So that Earth's flesh be freed from all suffering,
be clean as a whistle,
fresh as the body of a youth of fifteen years,
the landowners to a man were put to the sword,
and the lands and estates of the Sultan's men were shared
    by all.'

We heard . . .
How can we stay still when we hear such things?
One morning early
while a lost bird sang on Haymana plain,
we were eating olives under a stunted willow.
'Let's go,'
        we said.
'Let's see for ourselves,' we said.
'Let's put our hand to the plough
and cut a furrow in that friendly earth.'
We came to mountains and mountains,
we crossed them all . . .

Friends,
I don't travel alone.
One afternoon I said to my dear comrade,
        'We've arrived!'
        I said, 'Look!'
The land that one step behind us was weeping
has begun to laugh before us like a child.
Look at the figs like huge emeralds,
branches weighed down with amber bunches of grapes.
See the fish leaping in the wicker traps,
their wet scales gleaming, glistening,
their flesh white and tender
as a young lamb's flesh.
'Look,' I said,
'Human beings here are as fruitful as earth, as sun, as sea.
Here sea and sun and earth are fertile as human beings.'

5

Leaving behind us the fiefs, large and small, of the Sultan and the lords, we came into Börklüce's country, where the first to meet us were three young men. The three wore seamless white garments like my guide. One had a curly beard black as ebony, intense eyes of the same colour and a big curved nose. He had been one of Moses' followers. Now he followed Börklüce.

The second had a sharp chin and straight nose. He was a Greek sailor from Chios. He too was a disciple of Börklüce.

The third was broad-shouldered and of medium height. When I think of him now I compare him with Hüseyin who sings that upland folksong in the prison ward for brigands. But Hüseyin is from Erzurum, this man from Aydın.

He spoke first:

'Are you friend or foe? If friend, we welcome you, but if foe, your life hangs on a thread.'

'We are friends,' we said.

Then we learned that in the narrow mountain passes of Karaburun our men had overcome the army of Sisman, the governor of Sarohan, who was trying to return the lands to the Sultan's lords.

. . . . . .

Our joy in this news was great and my guide said:

'Let us go at once and give Bedreddin the news.'

So we took with us the Greek sailor Anastas from Chios, and left the friendly land whose threshold we had hardly crossed, and plunged once more into the dark lands of Red Osman's sons.

We found Bedreddin at İznik by the lake. It was morning, the air was damp and heavy with grief.

Bedreddin said, 'Now our time has come. We shall pass over to Rumeli.'

We left İznik at night chased by cavalry. Darkness came down like a wall between us and them. We could hear horses' hooves behind it. My guide led, then Bedreddin's horse between my bay horse and the horse of Anastas. We were like three mothers, Bedreddin was our child. We trembled for the harm they might do him. We were three children, Bedreddin was our father. We

closed round Bedreddin as the hoofbeats behind the darkness
approached.
Hiding by day, travelling by night, we reached İsfendiyar.
There we boarded a ship.

6

One night there were stars alone in the sea
        and a sailboat.
One night in the sea a sailboat was all alone
        with the stars.
Stars numberless,
sails slack.
The water was dark
    and perfectly smooth as far as the eye could see.
Blond Anastas and Bekir the islander
        were at the oars,
Koç Salih and I
    in the bow.
And Bedreddin,
    his fingers buried in his beard
    was listening to the splash of oars.

'O Bedreddin!' I said,
'over the sleepy sails
    we see only stars.
We hear no roaming breezes whisper,
we hear no tumult in the sea.
There is only the dark mute water
only its sleep.'
The little old man, beard longer than his body,
      laughed
      and said:
'Don't be fooled by the stillness in the air,
the ocean you say is sleeping is waking up.'

One night there were stars alone in the sea
        and a sailboat.

One night a sailboat crossed the Black Sea,
                on its way to the Mad Forest
                to the Sea of Trees.

7

Here where we stopped was the Mad Forest,
we pitched our tent in the Sea of Trees.
From every branch we flew a messenger falcon to every village.
We said, 'Everyone knows why we've come,
                everyone knows our heart's torment.'

Every falcon returned with a hundred lions in its wake.
The villager set fire to the master's crop, the apprentice the
        market,
                the oppressed came leaving their chains behind.
So all of us from Rumeli
                came pouring arm-in-arm
                        to the Sea of Trees.

A fiery tumult!
Men and horses, spears, iron, leaves and skin,
        beech-branches, roots of oak,
        mixed together.
Since it went mad
the Mad Forest had never seen such sights
nor heard such clamour . . .

8

Leaving Bedreddin and Anastas encamped in the Mad Forest my
guide and I came down to Gallipoli . . . . . . The journey to
Karaburun by way of İzmir was to bring news of our Sheikh to
Mustafa.

    When we came to a caravanserai near İzmir we heard that
Bayezid Pasha with his twelve-year-old son was gathering his
Anatolian forces.

    We did not delay long in İzmir. On leaving the city we followed
the Aydın road where we met four gentlemen resting and chatting

under a walnut tree in an orchard. They had dropped melons down a well to cool them. Each wore different clothes. Three had turbans, one a fez. We exchanged greetings and Neşri, one of the turbaned ones spoke:

'Sultan Mehemmed has sent Bayezid Pasha against Börklüce, who is inciting the people to join an unlawful and heretical sect.'
The second turbaned one was Şükrullah bin Şihâbiddin. He said:
'Many have gathered about this mystic Sufi. But their ways are clearly opposed to the laws of Muhammed.'
The third turbaned one was Aşıkpaşazede. He said:
'A question: if Börklüce were destroyed would he go in the end believing in Islam or not?
The answer: God alone knows his state in death. We can't know.'
The gentleman in the fez was a Professor of Scripture in the School of Theology. He looked at us closely, half shut his eyes and smiled slyly. He said nothing.

We immediately put spurs to our horses and in the dust of their hooves we left behind those men chatting under a walnut tree in an orchard, cooling the melons they dropped in a well. And we arrived at Karaburun and found Börklüce.

9
It was hot.
Hot!
That heat
was a knife with a bloody handle, a blunt blade.

It was hot.
The clouds were full,
the clouds were about to burst
                                and overflow.
Motionless he gazed:
like two eagles from the rocks
his eyes swooped on the plain;
there the gentlest, harshest,
                    thriftiest, most generous,

61

most
loving,
greatest, most beautiful woman:
EARTH
was soon
to give birth.

It was hot.
He looked out from the Karaburun mountains.
Frowning, he gazed at the horizon, the land's end.
A five-plumed blaze of fire swept the horizon,
plucked children's heads like blood-red poppies,
trailing their naked screams behind.
It was Prince Murad
who came . . .
He had been issued a royal decree
to go to Aydın
and descend on the heretic Mustafa, Bedreddin's caliph.

It was hot.
Bedreddin's caliph, the heretic Mustafa, gazed,
the peasant Mustafa gazed.
He looked without fear
without anger
without laughter.
Upright
and straight,
he gazed.
He gazed.
The gentlest, harshest,
thriftiest, most generous,
most
loving,
greatest, most beautiful woman:
EARTH
was soon
to give birth.

He gazed.
Bedreddin's stalwarts watched the horizon from the crags.
This land's end was slowly nearing
on the fateful wings of a bird of death.
Yet those who watched this land from the crags,
with its figs and pomegranates and grapes,
its flocks, their milk denser than honey,
and coats more golden than honey,
its horses slender-waisted, lion-maned,
had discovered this earth like a brotherly banquet
without walls or borders.

It was hot.
He gazed.
Bedreddin's stalwarts watched the horizon . . .

The gentlest, harshest,
                    thriftiest, most generous,
most
        loving,
greatest, most beautiful woman:
                                EARTH
                        was soon
                                to give birth.

It was hot.
The clouds were full.
Soon the first drop would fall on earth like a kind word.
Sudden-
        ly
pouring from the rocks,
                    raining from the sky,
                                springing from the ground,
like the last great work of this earth,
in seamless white robes,
                    bareheaded,
        barefoot and with swords unsheathed,
Bedreddin's stalwarts faced the Prince's army.

A mighty battle was joined.

Turkish peasants from Aydın,
        Greek pilots from Chios,
            Jewish tradesmen,
ten thousand heretic comrades of Börklüce Mustafa,
plunged like ten thousand axes into the enemy forest.
Their standards crimson and green,
        their shields inlaid, their ranks of bronze helmets
were all laid low, but
as the sun sank in pouring rain, by evening
of the ten thousand only two thousand remained.

Ten thousand gave eight thousand of their men,
so they might all together sing their songs,
and all together haul the nets from the waters,
and all together work the iron like embroidery,
and all together plough the earth,
all together eat the honeyed figs,
and all together say they share in everything,
                        everywhere,
except their beloved's cheek.

They were defeated.

The conquerors wiped the blood
                off their swords
                        on the seamless white robes
                            of the conquered.
That earth tilled by brotherly hands
like a song sung all together,
lay waste under the hooves
of the thoroughbred horses from Edirne's palace.

'But all this is the inevitable result
                of historical, social and economic laws!'
Don't tell me, I know!
My mind bows to your truth.

But my heart
does not follow such language.
It says
'O crippling fate,
O treacherous wheel of fortune.'
And one by one
in an instant,
            their faces streaming blood,
their shoulders striped by the whip,
Karaburun's defeated pass through the land of Aydın,
pressing on my heart
with their bare feet.

10

They stopped at dark.
He seized the word, he said;
'They've set up market in Ayasluğ city.
        But which of our friends,
                which have been beheaded?'

Rain
        was falling as if it would never stop.
They seized the word,
        they told him:
'The market is not yet set,
                but will be.
The wind
        is not yet quiet
                but will be.
He is not yet beheaded
                but will be.'

As soaking darkness fell veil after veil
I appeared where they stood.
I seized the word, I said:

'Where is the gate of Ayasluğ city?
                    Show me, I'll force it!

Has it a fortress?
Tell me, I will destroy it.
Do they exact tribute?
                    Tell me, I will refuse!'

Then He seized the word, he said:
'The gate of Ayasluğ city is narrow,
                    it cannot be entered.
It has a fortress,
                    not easy to destroy.
Go back then, young brave on your bay horse,
                    go back to your life!'

I said: 'I'll enter!'
I said: 'I'll burn it down!'
He said: 'The rain has stopped,
                    day dawns.
                    Ali the executioner
                        is summoning
                            Mustafa!
Go back then, young brave on your bay horse,
                    go back to your life!'

I said: 'Friends,
leave me be,
leave me be.
Friends
let me see him,
just let me see him!
Don't think
I can't endure.
Don't think
I can burn,
and not show the whole world how I burn!

Friends,
don't say
'It can't be done!'
Don't waste your breath.
This is no pear that will break from its stem,
even if bruised it won't drop from the branch;
this heart
is not like a sparrow,
            a feeble sparrow!

Friends
I know!
Friends,
I know where He is and his condition!
I know
he is gone and won't come back!
I know
his naked body
is nailed by his arms to a bloodied cross
on a camel's hump.
Friends
leave me be,
leave me be.
Friends,
let me go
let me see
Börklüce Mustafa,
Mustafa
one of Bedreddin's true men.'

Two thousand men to be beheaded;
Mustafa and his cross,
the executioner, the block, the axe,
all are prepared,
            all ready.

A red-embroidered saddlecloth,
golden stirrups,
a grey horse.

On the horse a heavy-browed boy,
Prince Sultan Murat of Amasya,
and beside him
Bayezid Pasha – I shit on his name!

The executioner wielded his blade.
Bare necks split like pomegranates,
like apples dropping from a green branch
        heads fell one after another.
As each head fell to earth
Mustafa from his cross
looked one last time.
As each head fell
not a single hair trembled.
    'Oh, my revered Sheikh,
      help me!'
          cried one,
and not another word . . .

I I

Bayezid Pasha came to Manisa, found Torlak Kemal there and
hanged him also. He inspected ten provinces where those who
had to be killed were killed, then the ten provinces were given
again as fiefs to the lord's servants.

I passed through these ten provinces with my guide. The
vultures hovered overhead, and uttering strange screams from
time to time they glided down the dark valleys and swooped on
the corpses of women and children whose blood had not yet
dried. Although the bodies of young and old men lay stretched
out along the roads under the sun, the birds preferred the flesh of
women and children, which shows how sated they were!

We met the regiments of the Sultan's lords on the roads.

They passed us as we left the ten provinces behind, through
winds that moved slowly and heavily over the ravaged land, like
the air in a rotting orchard. With their colourful banners and
plumes and their drums and song and dance the Sultan's servants
were returning to their fiefs again. Gallipoli appeared before us. I
said to my guide:

'I have no more strength: I cannot swim the sea.'
We found a boat.
The sea was stormy. I looked at the boatman. He looked like a picture I had stolen from the inside cover of a German book and hung over my bed in the prison cell, with his thick moustache black as ebony, his broad snowwhite beard. In my whole life I had never seen such a frank, open brow.

We were in the middle of the straits, the sea poured endlessly on, through the leaden grey air the foaming water slid under our boat, and our boatman who resembled the picture in my cell spoke:

'Freeman and slave, patrician and plebeian, feudal landowner and serf, master and apprentice, in a word the oppressor and oppressed, have always been in eternal opposition, and have carried on the struggle, sometimes openly, sometimes underground.'

12

When we set foot in Rumeli we heard that Çelebi Sultan Mehemmed had raised the siege of Salonika castle and had come to Serez. We began to travel both by night and day to reach the Mad Forest as soon as possible.

As we sat resting by the roadside one night three riders from the Mad Forest passed us at full speed, heading for the city of Serez. On the back of one of the riders' saddles I saw a shape like a man roped up like a saddlebag. The hair on my head stood on end and I said to my guide:

I recognize these hoofbeats,
those black horses in frothing foam
galloping full speed over the dark road;
that's how they always brought captives, bound to the saddle.

I recognize these hoofbeats.
One morning
                they came
to our tents like a friendly song.

We shared our bread with them.
The weather so fine
and hearts so full of hope
eyes became childlike
and our wise friend SUSPICION was asleep . . .

I recognize these hoofbeats.
One night
they sped at full speed away from our camp.
They had stabbed the watchman in the back
and bore on their saddles
        our best man,
                his arms bound behind.

I recognize these hoofbeats,
the Mad Forest knows them too . . .

We soon learned that in fact the Mad Forest knew these hoofbeats.

For as soon as we set foot on the edge of the forest we heard
that Bayezid Pasha had left men in the forest to penetrate
Bedreddin's headquarters and that they had treacherously joined
his disciples; one night they kidnapped our Sheikh asleep in his
tent and carried him off. The three horsemen we met by the
wayside were the fathers of all the provocateurs in Ottoman
history and the prisoner of war they had brought on the back of
their saddles was Bedreddin.

13

Rumeli, Serez
and an old phrase:
              'IN THE ROYAL PRESENCE'

Our elder
stood there upright
like a sword planted in the ground,
before the Sultan.
They looked each other in the eye.

The Sultan demanded:
'Before this blasphemy personified is laid low,
before the noose has the last word,
let the Holy Law show its skill
so the matter be rightly resolved.'

The learned council is ready.
A man of deep wisdom
his name Mevlana Hayder,
just come from the land of Persia,
bent his henna'ed beard to the holy script.
He resolved the matter,
saying:
      'To take his property is unlawful,
          to take his blood is permitted.'
      The matter is resolved.

They turned to Bedreddin.
They said: 'Your turn to speak,
          account for your heresy.'

Bedreddin
looked out through the arches.
Outside the sun shone.
In the courtyard a tree's branches had greened
and the flagstones were sculpted by running water.
Bedreddin smiled.
Deep in his eyes grew light,
          he said:
'Since this time we are defeated
whatever we do or say is vain.
Say no more.
But since the fatwa is passed on me
let me stamp it with my seal
and take it to my heart . . .'

14

Rain falls softly,
fearful
like secret whispers
of betrayal.

Rain falls softly
like the bare white feet of a rebel
running on dark wet earth.

Rain falls softly.
In Serez artisan market
across from a coppersmith's stall
my Bedreddin hangs on a tree.

Rain falls softly.
Late on a starless night,
swinging on a leafless bough
wet with rain,
the stark naked flesh of my Sheikh.

Rain falls softly.
Serez market is dumb,
Serez market is blind.
In the air the cursèd grief of the speechless and unseeing,
and Serez market hides its face in its hands.

Rain falls softly.

Şefik the Turner's Shirt

It was drizzling. Outside, beyond the prison bars, in the cloudy sky above the sea's horizon, morning dawned. I remember it well, even to this day. First I felt a hand touch my shoulder. I turned and saw it was Şefik the turner. The gleaming pupils of his coal-black eyes were fixed on me as he spoke:

'I don't believe you slept last night.'

Now there was no more rattle of chains from the bandits above. They must have dozed off as the sky lightened. The guards' whistles seem to lose their significance in daylight, colours are dimmed and their harsh lines which stand out only in the dark, soften.

The ward door was opened from the outside. One by one the inmates woke up.

Şefik asks:

'What's the matter? You're in a funny mood.'

I tell Şefik about last night's adventure. I say:

'I really saw him with my own eyes. He came to that window. He wore a seamless white shirt. He took me by the hand and I made the whole journey beside him, or rather, with him as guide.'

Şefik the turner laughs and shows me the window.

'I think you made the journey with my shirt, not with Mustafa's disciple. Look, I hung it up last night, it's still at the window.'

I laugh too. I remove the shirt from the bars, the shirt that belongs to Şefik the turner and was my guide in the uprising of the Kadı of Simavne's son, Bedreddin. Şefik puts on his shirt. All my comrades in the ward have heard about my 'journey'.

Ahmed says:

'So write about this. We need a Bedreddin Epic. And I'll tell you another story too and you can put it at the end of the book . . .'

So, at the end of my book, here is the story Ahmed told.

Ahmed's Story

It was before the Balkan war. I was nine years old, and grandfather and I were the guests of a villager in Rumelia. The villager had blue eyes and a copper-coloured beard. We drank tarhana soup with plenty of red pepper. It was winter, one of those Rumelian winters dry and sharp as a whetted knife. I don't remember the name of the village. But the gendarme who came and put us on the road told us its inhabitants were the most stubborn people in the world, the most pig-headed, the most unwilling to pay their taxes.

According to the gendarme they were neither Moslems nor infidels, perhaps they were Kızılbaş, or Redheads, but not exactly Kızılbaş.

Our entry to the village remains with me still. The sun was about to sink. There was frost on the road and red gleams in the frozen puddles glittered like splinters of glass. By the first village fences which were beginning to fuse with the darkness we were met by a dog. A huge dog looking larger than life in the half-light. It was barking.

Our driver reined in the horses. The dog leapt straight for their throats.

'What's happening?' I asked as I stuck my head out behind the driver. The driver's arm rose, his elbow struck my face, and the whiplash, hissing like a snake, came down on the dog's head. Just then I heard a husky voice.

'Hey, do you think you're the governor striking a peasant?'

Grandfather got down from the carriage.

'Hello!' he greeted the husky-voiced dog owner. They spoke together. Then the copper-bearded, blue-eyed dog owner invited us into his house.

Many conversations from my childhood still linger in my ears. I must have realized the meaning of most of them as I grew up, been surprised by some, laughed at some, and been angered by some. But in my whole life no conversation between adults has ever made such an impression on me as that between my grandfather and the blue-eyed villager that night.

Grandfather spoke in a soft, courteous voice; the other in a harsh, abrupt but confident voice:

'The naked corpse of Bedreddin who was hanged from a leafless branch in Serez in accordance with the Sultan's command and the fatwa of the Molla Haydar of Iran, was swinging slowly to and fro. It was night. Three men appeared from the corner of the market. One led a grey horse by its halter. A horse without a saddle. When they reached the tree where Bedreddin was hanging, the man on the left took off his shoes and climbed the tree. Those below waited with open arms. The man in the tree began to cut the rope, wrapped like a snake round Bedreddin's long, thin, white-bearded neck. The rope was wet and slippery; the blade of his knife suddenly slipped and pierced the neck of the dead man. There was no blood. The young man cutting the rope turned white as a sheet. Then he bent, kissed the wound and straightened up. He threw the knife away, and as most of the knot was already cut, he finished the rest by hand and delivered Bedreddin's body into the arms of those waiting below, like a father handing a sleeping son to a mother's embrace. They put the naked body on the barebacked horse. The man in the tree came down. He was the youngest. He came to our village leading the barebacked horse that carried the naked body. He buried the body under the elm on the hilltop. But later the Sultan's cavalry raided the village. When they had gone, the youth removed the body from under the elm, afraid they might raid the village again and find the corpse. He never came back.'

Grandfather spoke:

'Are you sure that is what happened?'

'Absolutely. My mother's father told me. And his grandfather told *him*. And so on. . .'

Apart from us there are eight or ten villagers sitting in the corners of the half-lit room painted golden by the stove. One or two move occasionally and as their hands enter this half-light, a part of their faces, a shoulder, turns to gold.

I hear copper-beard's voice:

'He will come again. The naked one hanged on the bare tree will come again.'

Grandfather laughs.

'This belief of yours is like the Christian belief. They too say that the prophet Jesus will come again to the world. Even among Moslems there are some who believe that one day the prophet

Jesus will appear in Holy Damascus.'

He did not answer grandfather at once. Pushing on his knees with his thick-fingered hands, he straightened up and now his whole body appears in the red light of the room. I see his face from the side. He has a big straight nose and speaks with conviction.

'They say the body of the prophet Jesus will be resurrected with his flesh and bones and beard. This is a lie. Bedreddin's body will come to life again without bones or beard or moustache but as eyes that see, a tongue that speaks, and breath in his bosom. I know this for sure. If we followers of Bedreddin don't believe in the next world or in the Day of Judgement, how can we believe that his poor decomposing body would come together again and be restored to life. When we say Bedreddin will come again we are saying that his words, his eyes, his breath, will come back again through our midst.'

He finished speaking and sat down. Whether grandfather believed or not that Bedreddin would return, I don't know. I believed it when I was nine years old and at thirty-odd I still believe it.

1936

A LETTER AND A POEM FROM
NURETTİN EŞFAK

Dear friend,
I'm writing you this letter in Ankara, in the Kuyulu Café.
The gramophone keeps playing the same old Anatolian airs
        from a mouth like a huge morning glory.
It's raining outside . . .
I've resigned from the school.
I've got a commission and I'm going to the front.
It's a fine thing,
            a great thing
to help our children to learn Turkish,
to teach them and get them to love
                their own language,
            one of the liveliest, freshest languages in the world.
But to strike a blow at the front for the people of this language
                        is greater
                        and finer.

I know:
        you are going to come up with 'division of labour'.
But to give lessons in Ankara to children,
to join the line of fire on the steppe
                    is a sad and unjust
                        division of labour.
We live in such times
that to say you've achieved something real,
you must always feel death breathing down your neck.

Look, just as I'm writing to you
soldiers go by in the street;
Their worn leather boots getting soaked in the rain,
they go down past the Assembly
                    on their way to the station.
A young Turkish peasant sings a folksong,
        a march in a high-pitched voice,
            as they always seem to do:

'Look at Ankara's stones,
Look at the tears in my eyes . . .'

Their faces serious, lost in thought and tired.
Beards a bit stubbly.
Their hands big and dark.
Hazel-eyed, dark-eyed, blue-eyed.

Once again Yunus Emre came into my head.
For me Yunus has another meaning:
I think that through him the Turkish peasant came
to a completely new language;
> not concerned with the next world,
> but with this world and its troubles.

I've written a poem,
a strange one,
called 'The Turkish Peasant'.
Does it seem odd to be writing poetry in times like these?
Well, anyway, goodbye,
> I embrace you.

> Your friend,
> Nurettin Eşfak.

THE TURKISH PEASANT

Shrewd without books
        he has learned from the soil,
he cries like Nasreddin Hodja
        he laughs like Zihni of Bayburt.
He is Ferhad,
        Kerem
        and Keloğlan.
When it's time to pack up and leave
he feels homesick and lonely,
his parents despair of seeing him again.
Backstabbing fate deceives him.
Floods sweep away Çarşamba city,
he loves a girl,
        another carries her off.
Broken-winged
        he strays in the deserts;
he is buried alive.
'Wretched Yunus
wounded from head to foot',
he drinks poison instead of water.
But if a wise man shows him the way,
and the right time comes
he will shout, 'Enough!'
When he says this –
'The Angel of Death will blow his trumpet
        and the whole of creation arise!'
Then earth's pulse begins
        to beat along with his.
He spares neither himself
        nor the enemy,
'he tears mountains apart
and cuts open rocks to make way for the water of life.'

'IN THE MOONLIGHT THE OX-CARTS WERE ROLLING'

In the moonlight the ox-carts were rolling,
ox-carts rolling on the road to Afyon from Akşehir.
The earth never ending,
mountains in the distance;
as if, though rolling on,
    they would never reach the overnight halt.
The ox-carts moved on with their oak-trunk wheels,
like the first wheels that ever rolled in the moonlight,
and in the moonlight the oxen
as though they'd come from some alien, miniature world,
were tiny, short,
and their diseased, broken horns gleamed
and under their hooves – the earth,
                    the earth,
                        the earth flowed.
The night was like daylight and hot,
and on the wooden beds of the carts
lay the dark blue naked shells.
The women with covert glances
looked in the moonlight
at the dead wheels and oxen from past convoys.
And the women,
our own women,
with their terrible, blessed hands,
        their little wasted chins, and huge eyes,
                our mothers, our wives, our loves
dying as if they'd hardly lived,
their turn always after the oxen
when it comes to eating;
and for carrying them off to the mountains we get thrown into
    prison,
hitched to the plough they work with the crops, the tobacco,
    firewood in the market,

and in the sheepfold they become ours
by the gleam of knives stuck in the earth,
with their frisky firm thighs
and tambourines for the dance,
our very own women.

'GALLOPING FULL-TILT FROM FURTHEST ASIA'

Galloping full-tilt from furthest Asia,
craning its mare's head to reach the Mediterranean;
        this land is ours.

Blood-soaked wrists, teeth clenched, feet bare,
and earth like a silken carpet;
        this heaven, this hell is ours.

Never again let labour be enforced,
let no man exploit another;
        this cry is ours.

To live free and single like a tree
and in fraternity like a forest;
        this longing is ours.

1947

POEMS WRITTEN BETWEEN 9 AND 10 AT NIGHT

(for his wife Piraye)

'How good it is to remember you'

How good it is to remember you,
in the midst of news of death and victory,
in prison
and in my fortieth year.
How good it is to remember you,
your hand forgotten on the blue cloth,
the dignified softness of your hair,
the dear Istanbul earth.

The happiness of loving you is like being reborn.
The smell of geranium leaf lingering on your fingertips,
a sunny calmness
and the invitation of a body,
a deep,
warm darkness shredded with bright red stripes.

How good it is to remember you,
to write about you,
to lie back in prison and think of you,
the words you said in such and such a place,
on such and such a day,
not the words so much as their world of expression.

How good it is to remember you.
I'm going to carve something out of wood for you again,
a little drawer, or a ring,
and I shall weave three metres of fine silk.
And jumping up from my bed
I'll cling to the bars of my window
and shout out what I've written to you
to the milk-white blueness of freedom.
How good it is to remember you,

in the midst of news of death and victory,
in prison
and in my fortieth year.

20th September 1945

At this late hour
in this autumn night
I am full of your words,
eternal as time and matter,
naked as an eye,
heavy as a hand,
words clear and shining as stars.

Your words came to me,
from your heart, from your head
from your flesh.
Your words brought you:
    they are: mother,
    they are: woman,
    they are: companion.
Sorrowful, painful, joyful, hopeful,
heroic, human words.

21st September 1945

Our son is sick.
His father's in prison.
Your head is heavy in your tired hands.
Our fate mirrors the world's.

Man will bring to man better days.
Our son will get well.
His father will come out of prison.
The depths of your golden eyes will smile.
Our fate mirrors the world's.

22nd September 1945

I'm reading a book:
         you are in it.
I'm listening to a song:
         you are in it.
I sit down to eat my bread:
         you're sitting facing me.
I work:
      you're facing me.
You, who are always ready and willing:
we can't talk together,
we can't hear each other's voices:
you are my widow of eight years.

23rd September 1945

What is she doing now, at this very moment?
Is she at home, or outside,
working, resting, or on her feet?
She might be lifting her arm,
O, my rose, that movement of your white, firm wrist
strips you so naked . . .

What is she doing now, at this very moment?
Perhaps she's stroking a kitten on her lap,
perhaps she's walking, about to take a step:
those dear light-stepping feet
that always bring my darling to me on black days . . .

What is she thinking about, could it be about me?
Or perhaps about the white beans taking so long to cook,
or why most of humanity is so unhappy?
What is she thinking about now, at this very moment?

24th September 1945

The best sea has yet to be crossed.
The best child has yet to be born.
Our best days have yet to be lived;
and the best word I want to say to you
is the word I have not yet said.

25th September 1945

It's nine o'clock.
The bell's gone in the compound.
They'll be shutting the cell doors soon . . .
This time I've been inside quite a time:
eight years.
Living is work in hope, my darling.
Living, like loving you, is serious work.

26th September 1945

They captured us, and threw us into jail:
me inside the walls,
you outside.
Ours is small business;
but the worst thing is,
consciously or unconsciously
to carry prison inside one.
Most people are in this situation,
honourable, hard-working good people,
worthy of being loved as much as I love you . . .

30th September 1945

It's a good thing to think of you,
it's a hopeful thing,
like listening to the best song
by the best singer in the world.
But hoping is not enough for me.
I don't want to listen to songs any more:
I want to sing them.

1st October 1945

Over the mountain:
a cloud laden with the evening sun over the mountain.
And today another day has passed:
without you, without half my world.
Red on red,
the night flowers will open soon.
Silent, brave wings carry our parting in the air,
our parting that is like exile.

2nd October 1945

The wind flows on.
The same cherry branch is never shaken twice
by the same wind.
The birds chirp in the trees:
their wings want to fly.
The door is shut,
it wants to be forced.
It's you I want:
let life be beautiful as you,
a friend, a darling . . .
I know the feast of poverty is not yet over:
but it will be.

5th October 1945

My darling, you and I know –
they taught us:
how to be cold and hungry,
how to be tired to death
and how to be parted.
But we haven't been forced to kill anyone
and we haven't been fated to be killed.

My darling, you and I know –
and we can teach them:
how to fight for our people
and how to *love*
every day with more soul,
every day a little better.

6th October 1945

The clouds pass heavy with news.
I crumple the letter that has
not yet arrived in my palm.
My heart hangs on the tip of your eyelashes.
The land stretches away in farewell.
I want to shout your name 'Piraye! Piraye!'

7th October 1945

Men's screams in the night crossed the open seas on the winds.
It's still dangerous to wander the open seas at night.
For six years this field has not been ploughed:
traces of tank treads remain as they were.
This winter the tank tracks are covered in snow.

Ah, light of my eyes, light of my eyes,
the media tell lies again:
that the merchants have closed the accounts they've sweated
    over
with hundred percent profit.
But those who return from the feast of the Angel of Death,
have returned under sentence.

8th October 1945

I've become insufferable again:
an insomniac, bloody-minded, stubborn.
Today I'm working, cursing and swearing,
flogging a wild beast,
then next day, see
how I'm lying on my back from morning to night
with a lazy song on my lips like a cigarette that's gone out.
The hate and compassion I feel for myself
take me right out of my suffering.
I've become insufferable again:
an insomniac, bloody-minded, stubborn.
I'm in the wrong as usual.
No reason: and there can be no reason.
I'm disgusted and ashamed of myself.
But I can't help it: I'm jealous of you, forgive me.

9th October 1945

You came to me in a dream last night:
you were sitting at my feet.
You raised your head and turned your huge, golden eyes
    on me.
You were asking something.
Your moist lips open and close,
but I can't hear your voice.

A clock strikes somewhere in the night,
as though bringing tidings of daylight.
There is a whisper in the air without beginning or end.
My canary in the red cage singing the ballad of Memo,
the crackling of seeds pushing forth
through the earth in a ploughed field,
and the triumphant, just roar of the crowd, I hear them all.
Your moist lips open and close
but I still cannot hear your voice.

I woke up depressed.
It seems I had fallen asleep over a book.
I think:
were all those voices your voice too?

10th October 1945

When I look into your eyes
the smell of the sunny earth hits me in the face,
I lose myself in a wheat field . . .
Your eyes are an endless canyon, sparkling green,
eternal matter, eternally changing:
releasing part of their secret every day,
but never surrendering completely.

18th October 1945

As we go out of the prison gate to meet with death
and turn to look at the city for the last time,
we can say this, my darling:
'You didn't give us much to laugh about,
we worked with all our strength
to make you happy.
Your moves towards happiness continue;
life goes on.

We feel good:
our hearts were content with bread that was ours by right,
in our eyes the sorrow of parting from the light,
we came, and now we are going,
good luck, Aleppo town.'

27th October 1945

We are half of the apple;
             this huge world is the other half.
We are half of the apple
          our people are the other half.
You are half of the apple
      the other is me
         the two of us.

28th October 1945

The lemon scented geranium in the pot smells stronger.
The seas roar.
Autumn is here with its full clouds and wise earth.

My darling.
The year is mature now.
It seems to me we have lived through a thousand-year
    adventure,
but we are still wide-eyed children running
hand in hand, barefoot in the sun.

5th November 1945

Forget the flowering almond trees.
It's not worth it.

Consider this.
You shouldn't think about things that cannot come back.
Dry your hair in the sun:
let its damp, red tresses gleam
like the languorous weight of ripe fruit.

My darling, my darling,
autumn is here.

8th November 1945

Your voice came to me, full and liquid
over the rooftops of my distant city
through the depths of the Marmara sea,
passing over the autumn lands.
A three minute call.
Then blackness on the telephone.

12th November 1945

The last *lodos* winds blew warm and roaring,
like blood gushing from a vein.
I'm listening to the air: my pulse rate is slowing down.
There's snow on the summit of Uludağ,
on the Kirezli pastures the majestic bears
are sleeping blissfully
on red chestnut leaves.
The poplars are stripping off in the plain.
The silkworm cocoons are ready for their winter quarters.
Autumn is just about over,
the earth is about to go to pregnant sleep.
We ourselves will get through another winter:
warmed in our great anger
by the fire of our blessèd hopes.

13th November 1945

They say, the poverty and hardship in Istanbul is
    unimaginable,
the people are broken with starvation,
TB has reached epidemic proportions, they say.
Little girls, in wastelands, in cinema-seats . . .
they say, were . . .
  . . . .
  . . . .
The news is black from my distant city:
city of honourable, hard-working poor people,
my real Istanbul.
My darling, this is the city where you live,
and wherever I am driven, in whatever prison I am,
this is the city I carry in a bag on my back,
that I bear in my heart like a father's grief for his child,
like the image of you in my mind's eye.

20th November 1945

Although there may be the odd carnation in a pot,
autumn has long since left the plain fallow,
and the seeds are being sown.
It's olive-picking time.
And time to enter into winter,
and time to plant spring seedlings.
As for me, I'm full of yearning,
and I lie in Bursa, laden, impatient for great journeys
like a tramp-steamer at anchor.

4th December 1945

Take out from the chest the dress you wore
the first time we saw each other.

Put it on, be like the trees in spring.
The carnation I sent you in a letter from prison:
put it in your hair.
Lift your high, white forehead
with its kissable lines.
On such a day you shouldn't be down and depressed,
it's not right.
On such a day, Nâzım Hikmet's wife should be beautiful
as a rebel flag.

5th December 1945

The hold has sprung a leak.
The slaves have broken their shackles.
The wind from the Polar star will blow up
and throw the boat on the rocks.
This world, this pirate ship, will sink,
sink inexorably, inevitably.
And we will create a universe, my Piraye,
as free, as light and hopeful as your dear brow.

6th December 1945

They are the enemies of hope, my love,
of flowing water, trees in fruit time,
enemies of the life which grows and spreads.
Because death has set its seal on their brows,
rotting teeth, perishing flesh;
they will be destroyed for ever.

My love, there is no doubt
that freedom in my beloved country
will go round, hand in hand, arm in arm,
in the best clothes of all,
the workers' overalls.

7th December 1945

The enemy to Recep the towelmaker of Bursa,
to Hasan the fitter in the Karabük factory,
to Hatçe the poor peasant woman,
the enemy to Süleyman the labourer,
the enemy to you, to me,
the enemy to any thinking person
is the enemy of the country, my darling,
the country which is home to these human beings.

12th December 1945

The trees in the plain are glistening their last,
scale on scale of gold, copper, bronze and wood . . .
The oxen hooves are buried softly in wet earth.
And the mountains are sunk in mist, leaden and dense . . .
It's over. Perhaps autumn finally ended today.
The wild geese fly past swiftly
probably heading for lake İznik.
The weather is cool,
there is a sooty smell in the air,
there is a smell of snow in the air.

Now, if I was outside
I'd gallop on horseback up into the mountains.
'But you don't know how to ride!' you'd say.
Don't laugh at me or be jealous.
In prison I've got a new habit
of loving nature
almost as much as I love you,
and both of you are far away.

13th December 1945

It suddenly started to snow in the night.
The morning began with crows scattering from snow-white
    branches.
Winter on the Bursa plain, as far as the eye can see:
no beginning no end fills my mind . . .
My love, the season has changed with a leap and a bound
after the struggle to develop.
And life goes on, confident and busy beneath the snow.

14th December 1945

Damn it! this winter's hard.
God knows what state you're in, you and my constant Istanbul?
Have you got coal?
Did you manage to get wood?
Block up the cracks in the windows with newspaper.
Go to bed early.
You say there's nothing left in the house to sell.
It's cold when one's half hungry and half full:
that's the lot of most people in this world,
in our country, in our city.

'IN ISTANBUL, IN TEVKİFANE PRISON YARD'

In Istanbul, in Tevkifane prison yard,
a sunny winter's day after the rain,
clouds, red roof tiles, walls and my face
      trembling in the puddles on the ground.
I am so brave in my spirit, so cowardly,
whatever there is, strong or weak,
      I carry it all,
I thought of the world, my country and you . . .

February 1939
Istanbul Tevkifane

1 'My darling'

My darling,
here's how it starts, the eyes wide open,
the red of burning cities,
the trampled crops,
and the tramp of boots going on for ever . . .

And men murder men:
       more easily,
       more calmly,
       and more
       than they do trees and calves.

My darling,
the tramp of these boots meant
I lost my freedom, my bread and you
in the massacre,
but amidst the hunger, the darkness and the screams,
I never lost faith in the days to come
that would knock on our door with sunny hands.

2 'I feel so happy I came into this world'

I feel so happy I came into this world.
I love the earth, the light, the struggle and the daily bread.
Although I know the circumference of the globe to the last
    centimetre,
and I'm not unaware that the world is just a plaything
    alongside the sun,
still, this world is incredibly big to me.
I want to wander the world,
to see the fishes I haven't seen, the fruit and the stars.
I've only made the trip to Europe in books and pictures.
I've never received a single letter from there
with a blue stamp franked in Asia.
My local storekeeper and I
are absolutely unknown quantities in America.
But so what!
From China to Spain, from the Cape of Good Hope to Alaska,
at every mile, at every kilometre I have friends and enemies:
friends to whom I've never said hello,
who could die for the same bread,
the same freedom, the same longing,
and enemies who thirsted for my blood,
as I thirsted for theirs.

This is my strength:
to not be alone in this huge world.
The world and its peoples are not a secret in my heart
nor an enigma in my mind.
Saving my skin from exclamation and question marks,
I found my place in the great struggle
with an open, untroubled mind.

But outside this place,
    the earth and you
        are not enough for me . . .
Although you are unbelievably beautiful
    and the earth is warm and good.

3 '*I love my country*'

I love my country:
I've swung on her plane trees, been inside her prisons.
Nothing dispels my depression
like her songs and tobacco.

My country:
Bedreddin, Sinan, Yunus Emre and Sakarya,
lead domes and factory chimneys
all are the works of my people
who hide from themselves and laugh
behind their drooping moustaches.

My country,
my huge sprawling country:
one could wander over it for an age . . .
Edirne, İzmir, Ulukışla, Maraş, Trabzon, Erzurum.
I only know the uplands of Erzurum from their folksongs,
and I'm ashamed that I've never,
never once crossed the Taurus mountains
to go and see the cotton-workers in the South.

My country:
the camels, the trains, the Ford cars, the sick donkeys,
the poplars, the willows,
and the red earth.

My country:
its pine forests, the freshest waters
and the trout that love
the lakes in the mountain tops,
who swim, scaleless and red-spotted
with their silver one-pound bodies in the Abant lake at Bolu.

My country,
the goats on the Ankara plains,
their long, glossy coats, chestnut and silken.

The heavy, oily hazelnuts of Giresun.
The crimson-cheeked scented Amasya apples,
the olives,
  the figs,
    the melons
and water melons
   and the cluster on
      cluster
of multicoloured grapes;
then the wooden plough,
  then the black flocks,
   then the hard-working,
honest, heroic people of my country,
ready to accept what comes, the good and all,
with a child's delighted acceptance,
half hungry,
 half fed,
  half slaves . . .

CONCERNING DEATH

Come on, sit down friends,
welcome, twice welcome.
I know while I was sleeping
you came into my cell through the window.
You didn't knock over the long-necked
medicine bottle or the red box.
You stood by my bed, companions together,
on your faces the starlight.
Come on, sit down, friends,
welcome, twice welcome.

Why are you looking at my face so strangely,
Hâşim, son of Osman?
How strange,
I thought you had died, brother,
in Istanbul harbour,
            loading coal on an English boat
                with your coal hod in the depth of the hold.

The boat's winch heaved your corpse out
and before the tea-break your bright red blood washed over
                                your coal-black head.
Who knows how our souls burned . . .
Don't stand there, sit down,
I thought you were dead,
you came into my cell through the window.
On your faces the starlight,
welcome, twice welcome . . .

Yakup, peasant from Yaya village,
        hello,
            my soul mate.
Didn't you die too?
Leaving your children to malaria and hunger,
one very hot summer's day,
weren't you buried in the leafless cemetery?

So you didn't die?

And you
Ahmet Cemil, the author,
I saw with my own eyes
          your coffin
               going into the ground.

And the coffin seemed
          a bit short.
Leave that Ahmet Cemil,
haven't you given up your old habits?
That's a medicine bottle
          not a rakı bottle.
To be able to hold on to fifty kuruş a day,
and to forget the world on your own,
how much you used to drink.
I thought you were dead.
Companions together by my bed,
come on, sit down, friends,
welcome, twice welcome.

An old Persian poet says:
'Death is just,
it strikes down the king and the poor man with equal majesty.'

Hâşim,
why are you shocked?
Have you ever heard, my brother,
     of any king dying in a ship's hold
               with a coal hod?

An old Persian poet says:
'Death is just.'
Yakup,
how you laughed, my soul mate.
You never laughed like that when you were alive.
But wait, let me finish what I'm saying.
An old Persian poet says:

'Death is just.'
Leave the bottle Ahmet Cemil,
no point in getting angry.
I know,
if death is just,
life has to be just, that's what you're saying.

An old Persian poet . . .
Friends, why are you leaving me?
Friends, where are you going
          so angry?

A BIRTH AND A FACTORY CHIMNEY

It was the ironworks chimney
           that stood
hopeless and vengeful in the rain.
The wind worked itself up and beat on the factory chimney.
While night was a black sail in the wind,
and trees were losing control of their branches, birds of their
      wings,
and earth was wrenching lightning from darkness,
and sidewalks were quit of people and tools
               and all were in deep sleep,
a child was born in a ground-floor room.

Stars came out one by one
        they burned in clusters,
stars like the child's eyes, bright
        with happy generous light.
The factory chimney glowed, smiled
and said:

'Know the one born in the ground-floor room, he is the one;
He is the guide and proof.
His mind is deep, full of pity, his wrath is fierce;
son of those without tools,
it is he who'll give tools to the needy,
he is the one in their midst, the one in the forefront,
in a night of mourning, a place of struggle, a day of rejoicing,
he is the one.
He'll hold them all in a mother's embrace.
To him the four ancient elements will submit,
earth, fire, wind and rain.

He will complete the last chapter of the story of the blind,
the son of man will write his own book,
          in knowledge,
              fulfilling his desire.'

The ironworks chimney was silent.
Dawn breaks.

THE DOOMSDAY VERSES

1 *The Verse of the Signs*

From the seventh subterranean stratum comes the roar.
Many signs have appeared, the time is ripe.
Impiety is rewarded, merit forbidden.
The white worm gnaws deeper at the black wood,
pump up the bellows
        the iron has entered the fire.

Many signs have appeared, the time is ripe.
It was noised abroad they made profit from death,
they disowned and denied themselves.
Rumour was, the chicken was tapping at its shell
and the giant with nothing to lose but his chains
was heard waking from his sleep.

From the seventh subterranean stratum comes the roar.
Don't look back, there's no help.
The bit cannot restrain the horse.
Do you see the rider's foot slip out of the stirrup
and his lip split, oozing blood?
Like this he rides on, still he rides on,
is there no halt on these fiery roads?
This is the road that ends there.
'How hard it is to turn into dust and earth . . .'

Pump up the bellows,
        the iron has entered the furnace.
A blazing chunk of metal has fallen amid the ice.
Signs have appeared, signs of Doomsday.
News is the seething water has reached boiling-point.

1939
Istanbul

2 *The Verse of Evaporation*

Stripped of all their garments, the wrestlers were naked,
each of their secret selves was revealed.
The vault of heaven was hot, there was a smell of blood.
Finally the iron reached the critical moment,
        the right degree of heat.

The poplars shivered and bent to the ground,
they knew their allotted term was come,
and the plane trees
        knew from the shrieks
that their roots like dead snakes
        were bursting out of the earth.
Stripped of all their garments, the wrestlers were naked.
On the rocks red-winged birds
        were ready to launch themselves.
They knew their allotted term was come,
the waves swelled and foamed
        they began to break.

The vault of heaven was hot, there was a smell of blood.
And wind
        rose slowly, it grew and grew,
and in a moment, in the twinkling of an eye,
'there came a sigh from the depths
the earth moved from its place.'
The arches of bridges collapsed,
the tombstones fell face-down and were hidden.

This is the moment of Doomsday,
this is the transformation of boiling water into steam.

LETTERS FROM A MAN IN SOLITARY

I

I scratched your name
with my nail, on the strap of my wrist-watch.
Where I am, you know,
there's no such thing as a mother-of-pearl penknife,
('sharps' are forbidden)
    or a plane tree, its head in the clouds.
Perhaps there's a tree in the yard, but
    I'm forbidden
to see the sky over my head . . .
How many are housed here apart from me?
I don't know.
I'm alone, far from them,
and they're all far from me.
    I'm forbidden
to speak to anyone but myself.
But I do talk to myself.
And as I find my conversation very boring
    I sing, dear wife.
What! you'll say,
that voice of mine is rough and out of tune
    but it touches me so deeply
        it breaks my heart.
This heart, like a barefoot orphan in those old sad stories,
    struggling through the snow,
his blue eyes wet,
his little red nose sniffing,
    wants to bury himself in your bosom.
It doesn't make me blush,
        this moment:
        it's so frail,
        so needy,
        and simply,
        so human.

Perhaps the explanation lies
in psychology, physiology, etc . . .
Perhaps the reason is –
    for months
    I've been prevented from hearing any other voice
    by this barred window,
        this earthenware water-jug,
            these four walls . . .

Five o'clock, my dear one.
Outside with its thirst,
    strange whispers,
    its mud-baked roofs,
    with a crippled and skinny horse
standing motionless in the midst of infinity;
outside, driving the man inside crazy from grief,
a scarlet evening with all its bag and baggage, all its craft,
descends on the steppe, on a treeless void.

Tonight will come suddenly.
Light will play about the crippled skinny horse.
Now in a moment stars will fill the treeless void
    of this no-hope nature
that lies like a rough male corpse before me.
Again we've reached the familiar end of the business.
Today too everything's in place, everything's ready
for a great nostalgia.
I,
the man inside
will show my modest skill again
with the thin piping voice of my childhood,
with an old simple song on my lips,
by God! which will still defeat my grieving heart;
I'll hear you in my head,
like watching you in a dim distorted mirror,
        so far away . . .

2

Outside, my love, the spring has come, the spring.
Outside, suddenly over the steppe
the fresh earth-smell, birdsong and all –
Outside, my love, the spring has come, the spring,
Outside, gleams of light on the steppe . . .
And now inside, the mattress alive with insects,
        the jug that doesn't turn water to ice,
and in the mornings sun on the cement . . .
The sun,
now every day till noon,
near me or far,
fading or radiant
        moves . . .
Day turns to afternoon, shadows fall on the walls,
the glass on the barred window begins to catch fire;
        outside it's evening,
        a cloudless spring evening . . .
Here inside, is spring's worst hour.
In short
the demon called freedom
with his glittering, scaly skin, his fiery eyes,
forces the man inside to submit, especially in spring . . .
This experience is always the same, my love,
        always the same . . .

3

Today is Sunday.
Today for the first time they brought me into the sun.
And for the first time in my life
I stood motionless in wonder;
      how far away the sky,
      how blue,
      how vast.
Then humbly I sat on the earth,
I leaned my back on the wall.
At this moment no daydreams,
at this moment no struggle, no freedom, no wife.
The earth, the sun and I . . .
I am happy.

LETTERS FROM ÇANKIRI PRISON (1–3)

I

Four o'clock,
        you're not there.
Five o'clock,
        You're not.
Six, seven,
next day,
and the one after
and perhaps
      who knows . . .

We had a garden
      in the prison yard.
It was fifteen paces long
        at the foot of a warm wall.
You used to come,
we'd sit side by side,
with your huge red canvas bag
          on your knees . . .

Do you remember Kelleci Memed
from the juvenile wing?
Square-headed,
with short, thick legs
and hands more massive than his feet.
He smashed a man's head
        with a rock,
for stealing honey from his hive.
He would address you so politely
        as 'elder sister'.
He had a garden smaller than ours,
        up on top,
          near the sun,
       in an old tin can . . .

Do you remember
one Saturday afternoon
            wet from the prison fountain?
Şaban the master-tinker sang a song,
– if you remember –
'Our home and country is Beypazarı,
who knows where lies our death . . . ?'

I've taken so many pictures of you
but you didn't leave me one.
I've only one photograph:
in another garden
            you are laughing,
            feeding the hens,
            so relaxed
            so happy.

There were no hens in the prison garden,
but we had some good laughs
            and were not unhappy.
What news we had
            of the best freedom,
how we listened to the footsteps
            of good tidings approach,
what marvellous things we talked about
            in the prison garden . . .

2

Sitting
one evening
at the prison gate
we read quatrains from Gazalî:
        'Night,
            the great deep-blue garden.
The whirling dancing-girls with their golden glitter.
And the dead full length in wooden boxes.'

If one day
far from me,
living oppresses your soul
like black rain,
              read Gazalî again.
And, my dear Pirayende,
I am sure
you will feel only pity
              for his loneliness, his despair
              and his awesome fear
in the face of death.

Let running water bring Gazalî to you:
'– On the potter's shelf, the king
is a clay pot
and on the tumbledown walls
are the victory inscriptions
              of Keyhüsrev . . .'

Leap upon leap.
Cold
              hot
                     cool.
And in the great deep-blue garden
              without beginning or end
              never stopping
              the whirling dancing-girls . . .

I don't know
why it's always in my head,
a sentence I first heard from you in Çankırı:
'When the poplar fluff blows away
the cherries come close behind.'
The poplars shed fluff in Gazalî,
but
the master doesn't see
              the cherries arrive.
That's why he worships death.

Şeker Ali is playing the bağlama up in the ward.
Evening.
Outside children are shouting.
Water flows from the fountain.
In the light of the gendarme station
are three wolf-cubs tied to acacias.
Beyond the bars
                my great deep-blue garden
                                has disappeared.
Life is the only truth.
Don't forget me, my Hatice . . .

26 *October* 1940

    3

Today is Wednesday:
– you know –
Çankırı's market day.
Through our iron gate will come to us
in our reed basket
eggs, bulghur,
and glossy, purple aubergines . . .

Yesterday
I watched them come down from the villages:
they were tired,
cunning,
                suspicious.
There was sorrow etched under their eyebrows.
The men on donkeys,
the women went by, barefoot.
Probably amongst them some you know.
Probably for the last two Wednesdays, at the market,
                they must have been looking
                for the 'modest lady from İstanbul',
                in the red headscarf.

20 *July* 1940

A CRACKED WASHBASIN

Süleyman's wife called him:
'It's me,
me, Fahire.
Don't you recognize my voice?
So I must have shouted.
Screamed?
Perhaps . . .
No, the children aren't ill.
Listen to me:
leave work and come,
only make it quick.
I can't tell you on the phone,
            it's not possible.
It's too long to wait till evening,
hours and hours,
too long.
Don't ask.
Listen to me . . .
If you don't find a ferry immediately
cross to Üsküdar by caique.
Jump in a taxi.
If you've got no money
get an advance from the boss.
Don't think of anything on the way.
Try and come without lies, if you can.
Lies are told to the strong
            and I am weak.
Don't mock me, darling.
Yes, it will snow,
        yes, the weather's good . . .
Come like the man whose heart I entered
            not like my husband,
like my big man, my clever one,
        come like my father . . .'

2

Süleyman came,
Fahire asked her husband Süleyman:
'Is it true?'
'Yes.'
'Thank you, Süleyman.
Look how calm I am now.
Look I'm not crying any more.
Where did you meet?'
'In a hotel.'
'Near Beyoğlu?'
'Yes.'
'How many times?'
'Three or four.'
'Well, was it three or four?'
'I don't know.'
'Is it that hard to remember, Süleyman?'
'I don't know.'
'So it was in a hotel room.
Who knows how dirty the sheets were?
I read in an English novel,
that hotels for this sort of thing
        have cracked washbasins.
Did yours have one of those, Süleyman?'
'I don't know.'
'Think then,
A light pink, flowery, cracked washbasin?'
'Yes.'
'Did you give her any presents?'
'No.'
'Chocolates or anything?'
'Once.'
'Did you love her very much?'
'Love her?
        No . . .'
'Are there others, Süleyman?'
'No.'

'You didn't have any others?'
'No.'
'So you did love her then . . .
If there'd been others
        I would have felt better . . .
Was she very good in bed?'
'No.'
'Tell me truthfully, see how brave I am . . .'
'I'm telling the truth.'
'They pointed her out to me.
She's like a cow.
Her legs are fatter than my waist . . .
But it's a matter of taste . . .
One more question, Süleyman:
Why?'
'I don't know . . .'

A snowy, heavy pine branch
at the level of the window in the dark.
A long time had passed since the hanging clock
in the hall had struck twelve.

3

Süleyman's wife, Fahire
        told her husband next day:
'The compassion I felt for myself
        was unbearably painful,
I decided to die, Süleyman . . .
My mother, my children and you ahead
        would find my tracks in the snow.
The watchman, the police and a wooden ladder
would bring up a woman's corpse
from the orchard well in the plot out back.
Is it easy?
To walk at night straight to the orchard well,
then pausing by the edge
to dive down into the darkness?

But I'm not just afraid
that my tracks in the snow
wouldn't be found.
The watchman, the ladder, the police,
the gossip, the shame,
the suicide of a deceived wife:
                              it's comic.
It's hard to explain why I died.
Who to? To everyone, you for instance.
A person, even when they've decided to die
                    thinks of other people . . .

You were sleeping in bed,
                your face calm,
sleeping like you always do,
before this and while this is happening.

Outside it had started snowing.
To go out on the balcony in just a nightdress:
pneumonia next day,
to die with no show of emotion.
No, I never thought of the possibility of catching cold.

I lit our stove.
First I had to really warm up.
My heart cracked like a tea glass.
I look at the window and the snow.
'The snow is like a bird who has lost
                        its mate,
it searches for past days and springs . . .'
My father loved that poem.
You don't like it.
'From right to left, left to right, trembling and fleeing.'

I went out on the balcony without turning off the light.
'. . . the snow like . . .
                    falls, falls, and cries . . .'
I sat on a chair on the balcony.
Not a sound in the air.

Snowwhite darkness.
As though I am asleep.
As though a man I loved very much,
fearful of waking me,
is padding around me.
I didn't feel cold.
My suffering became clear,
                    pure.
The light striking the balcony from the French window
was like a hot cloth on my knees.
I was thinking strange things
                in a lethargic sadness:
the plane tree on the Fener road
                is 150 years old, they say.
Insects who live only for a day.
The time will come
                when people will live
                        very long and happy lives.
People have hearts and heads . . .
People have hands.
People?
Where,
        when,
                what class?
Their people,
our people.
And despite everything,
the struggle for a new world.
Then you,
        I
                a cracked washbasin,
and the compassion
that I feel for myself . . .

The snow stopped.
Dawn was about to break.
I returned to the room
                ashamed.
If you'd woken at that moment

I'd have thrown my arms around you . . .
You didn't wake.
Yes,
thank God, I've not even caught a cold.

Now?
From time to time I'll remember,
from time to time I'll forget.
Again we'll live side by side,
and I'll be sure that you love me.'

    4

Six months passed.
One night husband and wife were coming back from the sea.
Stars in the sky, summer fruits on the trees.
Suddenly Fahire stopped,
looked lovingly into her husband's eyes
and slapped him as though she'd spat in his face.

16 *August* 1940

THE STORY OF THE WALNUT TREE
AND LAME YUNUS

We have a friend here,
from the Circassian
            village of Kavak.
Like great books he holds secrets.
He's interested
        in intelligent men
                news
                    puzzles of the mind.
His name is Yunus.
He lights our fires
            gives us water.
We talk about
            trees and days.
Probably the best
            days of our life
                        are still to come.
Now
        there was grief in our conversation:
                    of a walnut tree
                            cut down
                                and sold.

We know it well:
inside the courtyard
            it was on the left near the gate.
When he was six
            Yunus fell from one of its branches,
that's why he's lame.

Oxen love the lame,
for the lame walk heavily.
Oxen love the lame,
walnut trees don't love the lame,
for the lame cannot jump for walnuts,
for they cannot clamber up and shake the branches.

Walnut trees don't love the lame . . .

Our chats had a strange subject:
not all the unloved throw themselves
                              in the river.
We all have a lot of skills:
we can understand
loving without being loved.

Our chats had a strange subject,
a strange one:
            the story of the walnut tree
                        and lame Yunus.

It shed its walnuts in September,
its leaves stayed green till November.
When the Circassian road
            was lit up by the dawn prayer
            the branches awoke before the women.
Yunus passed under them lost in thought . . .

. . . Thinking,
            not a blessed task,
                        not a disaster
                                    not happiness;
and death:
            when you get there there's no return,
but for Yunus it was a village
            he never thought about . . .

It shed its walnuts in September,
its leaves stayed green till November.
its shade was treacherous in the sun,
it talked to itself in the wind
its branches looked down on Yunus . . .

. . . Why the stars go out in daytime,
why the world is round

and goes round the sun
                    Yunus did not know.
We told him these things
                    but he was not amazed . . .

It shed its walnuts in September,
its leaves stayed green till November.
It was high and spread abundantly.

Three people could not join hands
                    round its trunk.
If you sat under it at night
                    you couldn't see the stars.
And Yunus sat under it every night . . .

. . . Of Chinese Moslems,
and of the one-horned rhinoceros,
and the million microbes in one drop of water
                    Yunus had no conception.
The day we told him
                    he was not surprised . . .

It shed its walnuts in September,
its leaves stayed green till November.
Its roots deep in the earth,
darkness like water flowed over its top.
And Yunus passed under it every evening . . .

. . . One day as he was lighting our fire
                    and giving us water:
'You are our master,
                    we are your servants,' we said.
That did shock Yunus . . .

It shed its walnuts in September,
its leaves stayed green till November.
It used to talk to itself in the wind.
It was high and spread abundantly.

If you sat under it at night
                    you couldn't see the stars.
Darkness like water flowed over its top,
its roots went deep in the earth,
its branches looked down at Yunus.

'Village work is hard there's no doubt,
                    the body is beaten and crushed once only.
You squat on the earth and look in all four directions,
trying to guess where disaster lurks.
Surely it won't get you!'

But disaster struck Yunus where it hurt most . . .

'It's as though we haven't lived in this world.
We come,
            and we go . . .
Istanbul is a beautiful city I've heard,
I haven't had a chance to see it.
Why do thirty families out of sixty
                    have no fine goat's wool?
Yunus had none . . .

'Your words haven't
                    hit the target.
The world got on the train.
The world no longer depends on the ox's horns.
The ox is our hands, our feet.
It's very hard to sell an ox,
                    it's like killing half of you.
When the ox has gone, you'll know fear . . .'

Yunus' ox was sold . . .

'I suppose that's the end of the road.
I cannot make any sense of these things.
The land has turned to soap,
it slips from your hand.

All creatures have a lair,
            but the wolf has none.
If your land has slipped from your hand
            you have become a wolf without a lair.

The land slid from Yunus' hand.

It shed its walnuts in September,
its leaves stayed green till November.
Its shade was treacherous in the sun.
Ceaselessly Yunus
            thought about his loss,
while the tree, with its secret wish
talked to itself in the wind.

Children need a mother,
a seed the earth,
a man a woman . . .

Yunus carried off a girl:
for a wedding is expensive
            and to carry off a girl is cheap . . .
But the wife of a poor man is not strong . . .

And one day on the Circassian road
lit by the dawn prayer
            they were going along.
She collapsed behind Yunus,
and in her red headcloth she died there and then . . .

Landless, oxless and wifeless,
on their own in the world
            the walnut tree and Yunus.
Loneliness struck Yunus hard.
He sweated blood on another's land.
Thinking he had lost the walnut tree
in the dark, sleepless, he waited till dawn.

The walnut tree was indifferent to loneliness,
its roots went deep in the earth,
its branches looked down on Yunus . . .

They make chests of drawers from walnut trees,
what use is lame Yunus?

You have no shelter in winter's freezing cold.
They make chests of drawers from walnut trees.
How much more can you bear?
Yunus, sell your walnut tree.

It's no woollen blanket, you cannot wrap up in it.
They make chests of drawers from walnut trees.
It's just a lifeless tree, what's the use of it?
Yunus sell your walnut tree.

Do those who have, weave rugs for the have-nots?
poor walnut tree, o my poor lot . . .

There was a place for the wolf that had no lair.
They make chests of drawers from walnut trees.
It was half tree, half human.
Yunus, sell your walnut tree . . .

The corpse was naked, laid out on the snow.
They make chests of drawers from walnut trees.
They cut its branches, the branches were lopped.
Yunus sold his walnut tree . . .

Do those who have, weave rugs for the have-nots?
poor walnut tree, o my poor lot . . .

The morning does have a master.
The sun is not always in cloud.
Probably the best
                 days of our life
                         are still to come . . .

Now
there was grief in our conversation:
of a walnut tree
cut down
and sold . . .

LODOS

Beginning

Who knows how many million tons of water
                are tossing about in the ocean?
An empty tin afloat
                on the loneliest wave . . .

+1

For the last month prison nights have been like this:
female cats in heat,
moist thighs,
                bristling fur,
                mauled necks,
                        sometimes they cry like a bird,
                        sometimes like a human,
                            and they prowl
                            till they're pregnant.

It's nearly spring,
Lodos weather.
How violently it blows,
                how hot . . .

We are six hundred men
                without women.
They've stolen our chance to be fathers,
my most awesome power forbidden: to seed a new life,
to defeat death in a fruitful womb,
to create together:
my love, I'm forbidden to touch your flesh . . .

It's nearly spring.
Storm.
Lodos.

How violently it blows,
        how hot . . .
Somewhere another window broke,
        the third tonight.
Which empty ward door was left open
        to bang and thud?
        How it knocks!

+2

In Tepedelen,
a corpse at the front
under a blanket of snow,
his helmet flies from his head
        and rolls before the wind . . .

+3

In the factory yard
        an electric light
at the end of the fine wire
        swings to and fro.

A woman,
her neck bare,
her long hair and skirts flying
        at the workshop door . . .

The wind struck the beams,
from the workshop eaves
        a huge piece of ice fell to the ground . . .

.

+4

Galloping down to the plain: carriages,
bells on the horses' necks;
and the oil cloth flapping on their flanks
as they race to the sea at midnight . . .

+5

What's left of the poplars are long, stringy stems
                    lit up,
                    although there is no moon.
And the thick-branched, tangled chestnut trees stir
                    not rocking to and fro,
            but seeming to slowly, heavily change place,
the leafless, wooden throng
                    reaching as far as the eye can see
                    in the starlight . . .
But this *lodos*,
                    this roar,
and in the air
                    the smell of a woman's body,
                    and the fertile warmth of ovaries.
The snow melts in the mountains.
Sap runs
            right to the tip of the leafless branches.
Pregnant.
With child.
It's nearly spring
and the day of birth,
                    fearful,
                            beautiful,
                                    warm,
is upon us.

23 January 1941

A STRANGE FEELING

'The damson tree
        has flowered,
the apricot blossoms first
           the damson last.

My love,
let's kneel in the meadow
face to face.
The air is delicious and light
– but not yet really warm –
the almond shell
        is brilliant green and downy,
           still quite soft . . .
We're lucky
    to be alive.
If you'd been in London
and I in Tobruk, or in an English freighter,
we would probably have been killed long ago.

My love,
put your hands on your knees,
your wrists are white and strong,
turn your left palm,
daylight lies in your palm
        like an apricot . . .
In yesterday's air-raid about a hundred died
        under five years old,
twenty-four still at the breast . . .

My love,
I adore the colour of a pomegranate seed,
– a pomegranate seed, a sliver of light –
I love the melon's fragrance,
the tartness in the plum . . .

. . . a rainy day
far from you or any fruit,
spring hasn't unlocked a single tree
– there's even the possibility of snow.
In Bursa prison,
moved by a strange feeling
and a crushing anger,
I'm determined to write of these things,
in spite of myself and those I love.

7 *February* 1941

LETTER TO KEMAL TAHİR

When I say 'Malatya'
        all I see in my mind's eye are your stern brows.
There are hot springs in Bursa,
        apples in Amasya,
                in Diyarbakır melons and scorpions,
but what's so special
        about your place, Malatya,
its fruits or insects,
        its air or water?
I haven't even a clue, you know, about its prison.
Except:
there's one room
with only a single window
        near the very high ceiling.
There you are
        like a little fish
in a long, narrow jar . . .
My simile may not please you.
Especially these days
        when you must be comparing yourself to a caged lion.
You are right Kemal Tahir,
be sure, and I am too,
I'm not joking,
we are certainly lions,
        and what's even more wonderful;
                we are human . . .
We know very well our place in history, our class,
there's no difference between a glass jar and an iron cage,
        they're both the same,
        especially these days . . .
– But he who lies in prison safe and sound,
        knows this –
especially these days,
how to laugh at the stories of Emin Bey from Sarıyer,
the taste of beloved books and of tomatoes,

sleep despite bedbugs,
            – and three sweet spoonfuls daily of Adonille.
I can only allow myself the self-indulgence
of a letter from you,
Kemal, son of Tahir,
or hearing a voice, or touching, or seeing the air's light,
or loving my wife.
Pompous sentiments?
No.
To be unable to struggle;
to let the Mauser's bullet
            fly straight
                        to its mark.
You feel no pain if you're killed in the fight.
But of all freedoms the most important
is the freedom to engage in the fight.
I burn inside, Kemal,
            outside I'm cool.

You understand
what I'm saying,
            every one of our words
                        has often been spoken before,
                                    and will be again.
How many people, in how many places
are uttering these words now
in grief and cursing the hands that lie helpless, inert, on their
    knees?

You understand,
but never mind,
I'll say it again!
When you can do nothing,
            is talk and discussion the slightest consolation?
Perhaps yes,
Perhaps no –
but that's not the answer –
Give up consolation and religion, if you have it.

Do simply this;
head on, pace round and round on the spot,
roar, shout and bellow with rage, Kemal!

Autumn 1941
Bursa

A POOR NORTHERN CHURCH:
SATAN AND THE PRIEST

Morning began with rain at first,
then suddenly the sun burst out.
Left of the tarmac the field was still wet.
The prisoners of war had long ago started work.
Hating the earth
                – although most were peasants –
                    close-shaven and fearful
                          they were hoeing potatoes.
The chimes from the village church were reminiscent
of pale watercolours.

It was Sunday.
All the men in the church were old;
                    but not the women.
Among them were big-breasted girls
              and mothers whose fair hair had not turned white.
Their eyes were blue,
heads bent,
they looked at their thick red ruined fingers.
They were sweaty.
There was a smell of incense and boiled cabbage.
In the pulpit the Reverend Father
                  was reading 'the same old manifesto',
                – averting his eyes.

There was a stained-glass pane in the window.
Sunlight entering this pane
              rested on the snow-white nape of a young woman
                like an old bloodstain.

A child lay in the arms of a flat-breasted, slim-hipped Mary
              who had never
                  given birth,
        his head so big

and he so slight with his bent legs
he was pathetic and awful.

Before them an oil lamp was burning
lighting up
a hard
old
piece of painted wood.

The wooden statue was the height of two men.
Satan had hidden behind it
– his brows slanted, his beard pointed,
Mephistopheles probably –
and he listened with a learnèd smile to the Reverend Father.
' For the survival of Europe,'
(the Reverend Father was reading the same old stuff)
'we're fighting a war for Europe's survival.'

Satan was listening,
his pointed beard aggrieved,
the lie gave unbearable pain
to his rebellious and healthy mind.
The pastor was reading,
'Hand in hand with the European nations
we are fighting a war,
we will certainly eliminate
an element deadly to civilization.'

Satan pushed the statue of Mary aside a little
and tracing magic circles in the air
he raised his hand
to the priest
– a hand that was fleshless, and long,
bony and dry as the truth –
and at that very moment look what happened:
the woman below the stained glass window
appeared naked in the bright red sunlight.
Her breasts were heavy
and the hair below her belly shone like yellow silk.

The Reverend Father dropped his sermon
                    and tempted by Satan shouted the truth:
' The day to resist the greatest peril is come.
We are at war,
to keep prostitution alive,
and the doors of the brothels open.
And you there, standing at the back,
in your white garments,
like a little choirboy,
you'll become a whore, my girl.
And in one of our great cities
you'll get gonorrhea and syphilis.
Your father will not come back.
Now he lies face down
                    on foreign earth.
Now he lies bathed in blood,
                    his thick, fleshy ears,
                    his neck that your slim arms embraced.
Where he lies he is not alone
but on the field with motionless tanks and abandoned guns.'

Alarmed by his own words
                    the pastor was silent.
There at the back, a girl in white was crying.
A man in a velvet jacket
                    an old forest-warden from the neighbouring farm,
                    wanted to speak.
Satan scratched his pointed beard,
                    'Continue,' he said to the priest.
And the Reverend Father took up his sermon again.
' We are at war:
            to preserve property and trade.
            We the work-force must sell rubber, coal and timber,
to create more than its worth.
Cambric, petrol,
                    wheat, potatoes, pork
and heaven in a resonant young voice
                    must be sold.
The sunny garden and picture-books of childhood

the security of age
must be sold.

Health, honour and happiness
and
coffee beans,
all the goods of the market
                    must be weighed, measured, divided and sold.
We're fighting a war:
when we finish the fighting,
the hungry, the crippled and unemployed
              – but with their war-medals –
                    will be sleeping under the arches.'

Again the Reverend was silent,
again Satan commanded:
        'Get on with the story
        and tell them about the lad,
        what he was once and what he became.'

The priest continued:
        'You all remember him
        his childhood that passed
        like a potato seed in the earth
                    poor,
                        hard-working
                        and joyless.
He suddenly woke up
              at seventeen.
He was still poor, hard-working
but he discovered joy –
like suddenly one hot morning
finding a new world on the horizon,
after months
              on a cloudless sea
                    under limp sails
He had the finest voice in the neighbourhood,
              he was the best mandolin player.

And don't you remember
              the friendly warmth of his big red hand
              reaching towards you along the strings
              and the blue ribbons of his mandolin?
Whose heart did he break amongst you?
              To whom did he lie?
              Did he ever get drunk?
              Did he fight anyone?
Can we deny his respect for children,
              his kindness to the old?
Perhaps a bit thick in the head
              but his heart as clean as a new-born fish.
Last year we sent him to the war.
Now he is in the rear of the troops.
He's in the room of an occupied village,
busy raping an unconscious woman
              on a wooden table.
              His loins bare
              trousers at his knees,
helmet on his head
and short thick boots on his feet,
two dead children on the ground
              and a man tied to a pole.
It's raining outside,
from far away the sound of engines.
Pushing the woman off the table
              he stands and pulls up his trousers . . .
But you'll all remember him,
you remember him, don't you?
The friendly warmth of his big red hand
              reaching towards you along the strings
              and the blue ribbons
              of his mandolin?'

Again the Reverend Father was suddenly silent.
(It's a special skill to be silent
              if the words in a person's mouth
are not his.)

But behind wooden Mary
Satan again commanded:
'Father, continue –' he said.

And the priest went on:
'We're fighting a war;
        masses of manacled mankind
        forced to work
        piling chains on each other,
        must pour through cement pipes
        black and heavy.
And you, old woman
        on your knees in the front, on the left,
        your face wrinkled like parchment,
        I can assure you
                that your grandchild playing at the church door,
                        five years old,
                                his head round as a golden ball –
                        his grandad,
                                your husband,
                        his father,
                                your son,
                        will work in the coalmines
                                like your neighbours.

Let him learn
        to have no hope.
And so
our united bombers fly
and carry unimaginable numbers of deaths
                on their outstretched wings.
Perhaps they fill their engines
with a bit of grief
                as well as petrol.
(If such a thing can be imagined in murderers.)
Waves of our bombers fly
one after another
protected by fighter planes.

We're at war:
>the number of those we've killed
>– ours and theirs –
>amongst them children at the breast –
>at present
>>reaches five or six million.

We're at war:
>everyone's rank must be clear from their clothes.
We're at war:
>let the prison bars shine for ever
>in the morning sun . . .'

Reality is many-sided.
In a poor Northern church
>– even tempted by Satan –
>>a poor priest
>>>was unable to explain any further.
The military police got word
>>– from the forest warden in his velvet coat –
>>>they came and took the Reverend from the pulpit.
On the asphalt road
>as the Reverend father
>>left between two armed men,
Satan looked after him:
>hope in his slanting brows
>>grief in his pointed beard.

12 *September* 1941

NOTE:

Defeat of Germany;
the Reverend Father rescued from the concentration camp.
And if he had not been seduced by Satan
he'd be one of the big German democrats today
            in one of the Anglo-Saxon occupied territories.
But again he listened to Satan.
Again one Sunday and in the same church,
while praising and lauding the Western Allies
he repeated some of the things he had said in 1941
        especially concerning the laws of property.
By order of a Catholic American officer
        the Reverend Father this time was not arrested
        but chased out of church.
Again Satan's gaze followed him,
        with much more hope in his slanting brows
        and much less grief in his pointed beard.

17 February 1946

QUATRAINS

Part I

1

Hey Rumi, what you saw was the real world, not a 'mirage',
infinite, not created, a Designer not the 'Prime Cause'.
The most powerful quatrain left from your burning flesh
is not the one that says 'all Forms are shadows'.

2

My soul did not exist before her, nor is it a perfect mystery
    separate from her,
my soul is the image of her, she is my outer world reflected in me.
And the image furthest from the source and nearest
is my love's beauty shining on me.

3

The image of my darling spoke from the mirror
'She doesn't exist, I do,' it said to me one day.
I hit the mirror, it fell and smashed, the image vanished,
but my darling is right here, thank God.

4

Just once I sketched your image on the canvas,
a thousand times a day your picture filled me body and soul;
how strange, your image will stay there longer
on the canvas which will outlive me.

5

I can't embrace and sleep with the image you left me.
Although you are really there, alive, flesh and bone in my city,
your red mouth more longed for than honey, your huge eyes
    really there,
your surrender like foaming water and your untouchable
    whiteness.

6

She kissed me. 'These lips are real as the universe,' she said.
'This musky perfume flying from my hair is no invention,'
    she said.
'Look into the skies or into my eyes:
even if the blind cannot see them, still there are stars,' she said.

7

This garden, this moist earth, this scent of jasmine, this
    moonlit night
will continue to sparkle after I've trodden the earth and gone,
since before I came, and after I came they were there without
    me
and appeared in me just as a form of creation.

8

'That's it,' one day Mother Nature will say to us,
'no more laughter, no more tears, my child.'
The vast, infinite life will begin all over again,
a life not seeing, not talking, not thinking.

9

Every day parting approaches a little nearer
goodbye fair world
and hello
universe . . .

10

The honeycomb is full of honey,
like your eyes full of sun . . .
Your eyes, my darling, tomorrow will be earth,
the honey will go on filling other combs.

11

Neither from holy light,
                    nor from primeval mud,
my darling, the cat and the evil-eye bead round its neck
are all from the same dough – but different in their kneading.

12

The cabbage, the car, plague microbe and star –
we are all kith and kin.
And hey, my darling with eyes like the sun, it's not 'Cogito,
          ergo sum',
we exist in this splendid family and therefore we think.

13

We have only one degree of difference between us,
that's it my canary,
you're a bird with wings, that cannot think
and I'm a man with hands, who can think.

Part II

1

'Fill up your cup with wine, before it fills with earth,' said
    Khayyam.
Passing by the rose garden a long-nosed man in tattered shoes
    threw him a look:
'In the world with more blessings than stars, I'm hungry,'
    he said,
'I have no money for bread, let alone wine!'

2

Sweet sorrow to think of death and the shortness of life,
of drinking wine in the tulip garden under the moon . . .
This sweet sorrow was never our lot from the day we were born
in the slummy suburbs, on the earth floor of a pitchdark hovel.

3

Life passes, seize time's gifts before you reach the final sleep:
fill the crystal goblet with ruby wine, awake young man,
    it's dawn . . .
The young man woke in his curtainless ice-cold room,
it was the factory siren howling, unrelenting to the late for work.

4

I don't miss the past
                – except for one summer night –
but even the final blue spark of my eye
                will bring you good news of the future . . .

5

I, a human being,
I, Nâzım Hikmet, Turkish poet and communist,
I, made up through and through of faith,
of fight and longing and hope, from head to foot.

6

I, the announcer, spoke,
my voice as grave and naked as a seed:
    'I'm setting my heart to the right time,
    exactly at dawn the gong will strike.'

Part III

1

A human being
is either your admirer or enemy.
Either you'll be forgotten as though you never existed
or you'll never be out of mind for a single minute.

2

Biting into the firm flesh of a healthy white apple
one winter day unblemished, clear as glass;
O my beloved, loving you is like the joy of breathing
                                        in a snowy pine forest.

3

Perhaps we would not have loved each other
if, from a distance, we hadn't watched one another's soul.
We would not perhaps have been so close to each other
if fate hadn't parted us one from the other . . .

4

Now day has grown completely light like water
whose dregs have sunk, the rest is limpid clear.
My love, it's like suddenly coming face to face with you,
this light, this unbelievable light . . .

'BEFORE THE DAWN EMBRACES
THE MOUNTAINS'

Before the dawn embraces the mountains
and the waters catch fire with light,
haul in the nets, the nets.
Let our caiques collide
with the dark and let them fill
with flashing scaled fish.
Before the dawn embraces the mountains,
come on lads, haul in the nets.

1929
Istanbul

'I WANT TO DIE BEFORE YOU'

I
want to die before you.
Do you think the one coming after
will find the one gone before?
I don't think so.
Best to cremate me
and put me in a jar
      over the stove in your room.
Let the jar be a glass one,
of transparent, white glass,
      so that you can see me . . .
You understand my faithfulness:
I've given up the earth,
I've given up being a flower
      to stay by your side.
I am become dust,
I am living by your side.
Then, when you die,
you'll come into my jar.
There we'll live together,
your ashes in my ashes,
until a careless bride,
or a disloyal grandchild
throws us out from there.
But we
will mingle
together so
till then
that our particles when thrown out in the rubbish
will fall side by side.
We'll go deep together into the earth.
And if one day a wild flower
from this dampened earth shoots forth
there will definitely

be two flowers on its stem
                    one you,
                    one me.

I
don't think any more about death.
I shall have another baby.
Life flows from me.
My blood seethes.
I shall live, yes indeed,
but together with you.
But death doesn't make me afraid.
But I don't like at all
                    our form of funeral.
Perhaps before my death
it will have changed for the better.
Is there a possibility of your coming
out of prison one of these days?
Something inside says:
                    yes, perhaps.

18 *February* 1945
Piraye Nâzım Hikmet

'SUPPOSE ISTANBUL MY HOMETOWN SENT ME A CYPRESS CHEST'

Suppose Istanbul my hometown sent me a cypress chest by sea
to be delivered by trusty Nuri Efendi,
a bride's chest,
and I opened the lid which would sing like a tinkling bell:
        'Two bales of linen from Şile,
        two pairs of raw-silk shirts,
        muslin handkerchiefs, silver-worked,
        sweet-scented soaps from Edirne,
        gauze bags of lavender
                and YOU' appeared.
I'd seat you on the edge of my bed,
and spread my wolfskin under your feet
and stand before you, hands clasped in respect,
deeply humble,
and look in your face with admiring wonder.

My God, how lovely you are!
Istanbul's air and water are in your laugh,
Istanbul's delights in your look.

O my sovereign mistress, if you permit
and your slave Nâzım Hikmet has the courage,
he'll kiss you and smell you and it will seem
like kissing and smelling Istanbul's cheek.

But beware,
don't say to me, 'Come!'
If my hand touches yours I can't bear it,
        I think I'd keel over on the concrete
                from shock and die.

        . . . .

What strange things I'm writing to you, my darling,
when I can just send a telegram simply saying 'I love you'.

1945

A SPRING SCENE

On elbows and knees
    he crawled through the field like a four-legged crippled animal.
The strap on his automatic had ridden up to his neck.
His face and hands were filthy.
His back stretched in despair.

The ice had broken up a month ago.
With a terrible crashing the gleaming masses
       had flowed down the rivers to warm seas.
First, it had rained for fifteen days,
then suddenly the night before
    the clouds had dispersed,
       the stars had suddenly grown hot
    and had come so close to men,
       that if you stretched out
    you could light your cigarette from their fire.

He was crawling over the wet earth.
His nose was bleeding.

There was one hour till daybreak,
but the air was luminous as though night would never come again.
Seeds in water and earth,
      farewell to your long sleep!
Insects had multiplied,
soon the wild geese would fly from south to north.

He had let his beard grow.
He was as old as a plant and his head under his heavy helmet
      was of indeterminate age.
Only his teeth were like those of a young wolf, white and clean.
There were promises in the air,
the earth was laden with promises given.
Living was happy even for frogs.

The frogs were soft and nimble,
joyful with their wide mouths and thin legs,
        frogs leaping about in the wet field.

Suddenly on his four legs he stopped
and looked at the leaping frogs.
Blood dripped from his nose on the automatic.

It was spring, my darling, spring,
and everything was ready,
        ready to be happy,
                in the earth, air, water
                        everything.

1945

'I SHUT MY EYES TIGHT'

I shut my eyes tight:
you are there in the dark,
lying on your back in darkness,
your forehead and wrists are a golden triangle in the dark.

My darling, you are inside my eyelids that are closed,
there are songs inside my closed eyelids.
Now everything starts with you in there.
Now, there is nothing there that was mine before you
and nothing that doesn't belong to you.

1947

IN BURSA'S FORTRESS PRISON

Your lover is a communist
a prisoner for ten years
in Bursa's fortress prison.

But the prisoner broke his chains
his captive spirit soared
in Bursa's fortress prison.

Rooted in his country's soil
like Bedreddin he bears his load
in Bursa's fortress prison.

His heart undaunted, buoyant,
singing still,
his paradise not lost
in Bursa's fortress prison.

1947

THE WEIRDEST CREATURE IN THE WORLD

Brother, you're like a scorpion,
a scorpion in a cowardly darkness.
Brother, you're like a sparrow,
caught in the sparrow's flurry.
Brother, you're like a mussel,
closed and at ease like a mussel.
And, brother, you are terrifying like the mouth of an extinct
    volcano.

What a pity,
            you're not one or five,
                    there are millions of you.
Brother, you're like sheep,
when the cattle-dealer, dressed in sheepskin, raises his cudgel
            you join the herd at once
and you run, almost proudly, to the slaughterhouse.
All this means you are the weirdest creature in the world,
you're even stranger than the fish
            that knows nothing of the sea although it swims through it.
And this tyranny in the world
                    is all because of you.
And if we're hungry and tired and drenched in blood,
and if we keep getting crushed like grapes to provide your wine
                    it's all your fault
                        – it's hard for me to say so
                    but much of that fault, dear brother, is yours.

1947

ILLUSTRATION ON THE COVER
OF A POETRY BOOK

'You know the painter and poet, Bedri Rahmi. I like his paintings very much and particularly those where he uses our Turkish folk motifs. Recently I became absorbed for a whole hour (that's no exaggeration) before an illustration of his on the cover of a book of poetry; it was like listening intently to a song or reading a book or something like that. Later on I sent that book to my son. Two months went by and a desire to see that picture again awoke in me and I wrote a strange piece that brought it back to mind. Here it is:—'

[From a letter written in prison to Kemal Tahir, 1947]

Here comes the desert, with tracks in its sand;
here comes the Pole, dumb, with its white ice;
here comes the sea with its salt;
and the smooth level plains
where the lean-waisted greyhound
                    races with the sky.
Here comes Diyarbakır at night
emerging from the fortress
and at night the shores of the Tigris
                    crackle with watermelons bursting open.
With its chattering birds comes the plane tree,
the fish comes with its sea
and its silvery scales.
The ship comes with her star
and the mermaid beside the arching prow.
Here comes beauty with her shy gazelle look;
the snake with its crimson eye;
here comes mankind with dusty feet,
mankind with two words of passion.
And Nâzım says: here comes Bedri, son of Eyyub,
                    his neck long, submissive,
                    with his greens and reds,
                    his silver lines
                    and with his strange writing . . .

1947

ULUDAĞ

For seven years we've been staring at each other, face to face,
the mountain never moves from its place
                              nor do I
yet we're closely acquainted.

Really like every living thing, it knows how to laugh and be angry.

Sometimes,
        especially in winter, specially at night,
                and specially when the wind blows from the south,
with its snowy pine woods, upland pastures and frozen lakes
                        it stirs a little in sleep.
And the Monk who lives up there at the summit,
                        his long beard in disarray,
                                his skirts flying,
comes down to the plain shouting and yelling before the wind.

Then sometimes,
        specially in May, at daybreak,
        deep blue, boundless, massive,
                it rises like a brave new world
                happy and free.

But some days,
                it's like the pictures on lemonade bottles.
And I know in the hotel invisible to me
                there are women skiers drinking cognac,
                flirting and laughing with their men.

And some days,
one of the dark-browed men from the mountains
in his coarse yellow baggy trousers
slaughters his neighbour in the Holy Place of the mosque
and comes to us as a guest
to stay in prison in cell 71 for fifteen years.

1947

DON QUIXOTE

In his fiftieth year
the knight of immortal youth
in tune with the impulse
    beating in his heart,
set off one July morning to conquer
    justice, beauty, truth:
before him the world
with its spiteful, stupid giants,
    beneath him his sad heroic Rozinante.

This I know,
above all beware
of succumbing to absolute longing,
and beware your stalwart heart,
there's no escape, my friend, Don Quixote, no escape:
the windmills must be fought.

You are right,
on the face of the earth
the most beautiful woman is surely your Dulcinea,
and this you will surely shout in the face of merchants
who'll drag you down
and give you a proper beating.
But you, invincible knight of our drought and thirst,
you will continue to burn, a flame,
    in your massy shell of iron,
and Dulcinea's beauty will multiply more and more . . .

1947

ON LIVING

I

Life's no joke,
you must live it in earnest
        like a squirrel, for example,
expecting nothing outside your life or beyond,
        you must concentrate wholly on living.

You must take living seriously,
so much so that,
your back to the wall, your arms bound behind;
or in a laboratory
        in your white coat and big goggles
        you can die for mankind,
        even for people whose faces you've never seen,
        even though nobody forces you,
        even though you know the best thing, the most real,
                is to live.

You'll take living so seriously,
that even at seventy you'll plant olive trees
not just to leave to your children;
        but because, although you fear death
                you don't believe in it,
                so great is the power of life.

1947

II

Say we're ill enough for a major operation,
I mean that perhaps we won't ever get up
    from the white table.
If we have to feel sorry for leaving a little early,
we can still laugh at Nasreddin Hodja jokes,
and look from the window to see if it rains,
or hang around restless
    for the latest news.

Say we're fighting for something worthwhile,
    at the front, for example;
at the first assault the first day,
    we might fall face down and die.
We'll feel a strange anger,
    and not knowing
    the end of that war which could last for years
    will still drive us mad.

Say we're in prison,
our age almost fifty,
eighteen years till they open the iron door;
but we must still live with the world outside,
with its people and animals, its quarrels, its wind,
    the world beyond the wall.

But wherever, however we are,
    we must live as though
    we will never die.

1948

III

This world will grow cold,
a star among stars,
            one of the smallest,
this great world of ours
            a gilded mote on blue velvet.

This world will grow cold one day,
not even as a heap of ice,
or a lifeless cloud,
it will roll like an empty walnut round and round
            in pitch darkness for ever.

For now you must feel this pain,
and endure the sadness,
but so love this world
            that you can say,
            'I have lived'.

February 1948
[*Letter to Kemal Tahir from prison*]

ANGINA PECTORIS

If half my heart is here,
        half of it is in China, doctor.
It's in the army flowing to the Yellow river.
Then, at every dawn, doctor,
        at every dawn, my heart
                is riddled with bullets in Greece.

Then when our convicts get to sleep
      retreating from the ward
           my heart is in a broken down old manor in Çamlıca,
                        every night,
                        doctor.

Then for all those ten years
all I have to offer my poor people
      is this one apple I hold, doctor,
                a red apple:
                  my heart . . .

It's not from arteriosclerosis, nor nicotine, nor prison,
that I have this angina pectoris,
      but because, dear doctor, because of this.

I look at night through iron bars,
despite the pressure in my chest,
my heart beats along with the farthest star.

April 1948

OCCUPATION

As day breaks over the horns of my oxen
I plough the earth with patient pride.
On my bare feet the earth is moist and warm.

My biceps gleaming,
I hammer iron till noon,
darkness is stained red.

In the afternoon heat I gather olives,
their leaves the most beautiful green.
My clothes, my eyes and face, are steeped in light.

Every evening without fail I have a guest,
my door is open wide
                    to all his songs.

By night, kneedeep I enter the water,
I haul nets from the sea:
stars and fish mingled together.

I am called to account
for the state of the world:
people and earth, darkness and light.

But you know, I'm up to my eyes in work,
surely, my rose, you know
I am wholly preoccupied with loving you.

1948

AUTUMN

The days are gradually getting shorter,
the rains are about to start.
My door waited wide open for you.
               Why were you so late?

Bread, salt, a green pepper on my table.
Waiting for you
I drank on my own
half the wine I kept for you in my jug.
               Why were you so late?

But look, the honeyed fruit,
ripe on the branch, remains alive.
If you had been any later
it would have dropped unplucked to the ground.

ADVICE FOR SOMEONE GOING INTO PRISON

If instead of getting the rope
    you're thrown inside
    for not cutting off hope
    from your world, your country, your people;
    if you do a ten or fifteen year stretch,
    or more than the time you have left
don't say:
    'Better to have swung at the end of a rope like a flag.'
You must insist on living.

There may not be happiness
but it is your binding duty
        to resist the enemy,
        and live one extra day.

Inside, one part of you may live completely alone
        like a stone at the bottom of a well.
But the other part of you
    must so involve yourself
    in the whirl of the world,
    that inside you will shudder
when outside a leaf trembles on the ground forty days away.

Waiting for a letter inside,
singing melancholic songs,
staying awake all night, eyes glued to the ceiling,
    is sweet but dangerous.

Look at your face from shave to shave,
forget how old you are,
protect yourself from lice, and from spring evenings,
    and eat your bread to the very last crumb
and don't ever forget the freedom of laughter.

Who knows,
if the woman you love no longer loves you,
it's no small thing,
it's like the breaking of a fresh green twig
                    to the man inside.

Inside it's bad to think of roses and gardens.
It's good to think of mountains and oceans.
Never stop reading and writing,
and I recommend you weaving
and silvering mirrors.

What I'm saying is that inside, ten years or fifteen years
                    or even more can be got through,
they really can:
          enough that you never let the precious stone
          under your left breast grow dull.

May 1949

YOUR HANDS AND THE LIES

Your hands: dignified as stones,
sad as songs sung in prison,
clumsy and heavy as beasts of burden,
your hands like the cross faces of hungry children.

Light and nimble as bees,
heavy as milk-laden breasts,
brave as nature,
your hands hiding their friendly softness under their skin,
soft in friendship.

This world does not depend on ox horns,
                your hands hold up the world.

Mankind, oh my people,
they feed you on lies.
Although you're hungry
and in need of feeding with meat and bread,
not having eaten your fill even once from a white tablecloth
you flee like refugees from this world
where every branch bears fruit.

Mankind, oh my people,
Asians, Africans,
       Near Easterners, Middle Easterners, Pacific Islanders
                   and my fellow countrymen,
that is more than seventy percent of all people:
like your hands you're old, absent-minded,
like your hands you're curious, enthusiastic, young.

Mankind, oh my people,
my Europeans, my Americans,
like your hands you are wide awake, bold and forgetful,
like your hands you're quick to be conned,
                    easily taken in.

Mankind, oh my people,
if the radio tells lies,
if the press tells lies,
if books tell lies,
if posters on the walls, ads in the columns tell lies,
if the naked calves of girls on the white screen tell lies,
if prayers tell lies,
if lullabies tell lies,
if dreams tell lies,
if the violin player at the tavern tells lies,
if the moonlight of nights' hopeless days tells lies,
if the word tells lies,
if colour tells lies,
if the voice tells lies,

if everyone and everything you lived by
                apart from your hands
                        tell lies,
it's so that your hands may be malleable as moist clay,
your hands be blind as darkness,
your hands be dumb as a sheepdog,
                so that your hands may not make revolution.
It's so that in this life and death world,
        where we are guests for so little time
        this empire of grasping and oppression should not end!

1949

FIVE DAYS INTO THE HUNGER STRIKE

My friends,
please forgive me
if I cannot say properly
what I want to say.
I'm a little drunk, a little light-headed,
        not from rakı
        but from starvation's medicine.

My friends,
Europeans, Asians, Americans,
I, in this month of May,
    am neither in prison, nor on hunger strike:
    I'm lying in a meadow at night,
    your eyes like stars at my bedhead,
and your hands like one hand in my palm,
    like my mother's hand,
     like my loved one's hand,
      like Memet's hand,
       like life's hand.

My friends,
you have never abandoned me,
    not me, nor my country, nor my people.
I know your love for me and mine
    is like my love for you and yours.
        For this my friends, I thank you, I thank you.

My friends,
I have no intention of dying.
I know,
    I'll continue to live still in your minds.

I'll be in a line of Aragon,
      'in every line that tells of the beautiful days to come,'
      and in Picassos's white dove,
          and Paul Robeson's songs,
     and most beautiful of all,
         I will be your companion smiling in victory
along with the dockers of Marseilles.

My friends,
I'm so happy,
over the moon with happiness,
and that's the truth.

May 1950

SAD FREEDOM

You sell out – your eyes' alertness, the radiance of your hands.
You knead the dough of the bread of life, yet never taste
    a slice.
You are a slave working in your great freedom.
You are free
with the freedom to suffer hell to make Croesus rich.

As soon as you're born work and worry,
windmills of lies are planted in your head.
You hold your head in your hands in your great freedom.
You are free
in your freedom of conscience!

You are decapitated.
Your arms loll at your sides.
You wander the streets in your great freedom.
You are free
in your great freedom of being out of work!

You love your country as your dearest love,
but one day, for instance, you could sign it over to America
together with your great freedom.
You are free
in your freedom to become its airbase.

Wall Street grabs you by the scruff of your neck.
One day they could send you to Korea.
You could fill a pit with your great freedom.
You are free
with the freedom of being the unknown soldier.

You say you should live like a human being,
not a tool, a number, a means to an end.
They clap on the handcuffs in your great freedom.
You are free
in your freedom to be arrested, go to prison, even be hanged.

In your life there are no iron, bamboo or lace curtains.
There's no need to choose freedom:
you are free.
This freedom is a sad thing beneath the stars.

1951

TESTAMENT

Friends, if it's not my lot to see the day
of independence, dying before it,
take me away,
bury me in a village graveyard in Anatolia.

Let Osman who worked the fields lie on one side
                   – Hasan Bey had him killed –
on my other Ayşe, victim of war who gave birth
in the rye field
and died before her forty days were over.

Let there be singing and tractors near the graveyard,
young people at daybreak, the scorched smell of petrol,
fields owned in common, water in the channels,
no droughts or fear of gendarmes.

It's certain we will never hear those songs.
The dead lie underground full length,
                  they decay like black branches
underground, deaf, blind and dumb.

But I sang all those songs
                before they were recorded,
I knew the scorched smell of petrol
before tractors were ever designed.

As to my silent neighbours,
Osman the labourer, Ayşe who died in wartime,
they missed so much in their lives
and perhaps hardly noticed what they felt.

Friends, if I die before that day,
– and it seems I will –
bury me in a village graveyard in Anatolia,

and if it's fitting
and a plane tree grows at my head,
then there's no need for a gravestone or anything else . . .

27 April 1953

EVENING

Evening on the Hungarian plain
sky-blue
  pink
   pale purple
is just like evening on the plains of Anatolia.
The trees are trees we know, they grow on our plains.
Under the trees
    in the cool of evening
the earth is like a soldier's cape
    hot and damp with sweat.
The earth is like a soldier's cape
the same colour
    just as boundless
     enduring for ever,
evening on the Hungarian plain
is just like evening on the plains of Anatolia.
Stars perch in branches
    among the leaves
     with the birds,
the trees are trees we know, they grow on our plains.
Evening, the earth and trees
    seem alike so far.
But on our plains children are hungry,
    brides are old women at twenty,
the oxen are only one span in height.
Our plains are not Hungary's plain.

30 *March* 1954

THE POSTMAN

In the early morning
                or
                        middle of the night
I brought people news in my mailbag heart,
news of home and country, the world and its folk,
news of a tree, of bird and beast.
I went in for poetry,
                a kind of postal service, after all.
As a child I'd wanted to be a postman,
not as a writer of poetry and such, but
a real live postman.
A thousand different pictures were pencilled in colour
through Jules Verne's novels to geography books,
but the picture of Nâzım the postman
                was always the same.
So here am I riding a dog-driven sledge
                on the ice.
The northern daybreak glimmers
                on canned food.
I'm crossing the Bering Straits.
Or here on the steppe under looming clouds,
the soldier's letter delivered, I'm drinking ayran;
or on a mighty city's humming pavement,
only good news in my bag,
                only letters of hope.
Or I'm in the desert, under the stars.
A little girl is ill with fever.
At midnight a knock on the door:
                – the Post!
The child's eyes open wide, deep blue.
Tomorrow night her father comes home from prison.
I was the one who found the house in that furious snowstorm,
the neighbour who brought the telegram to the girl.
As a child I'd wanted to be a postman.
But in my Turkey to be a postman's a difficult art.

In my wonderful country the postman brings
               telegrams of many kinds of pain,
               letters line after line of grief.
Now in my fifties I've reached my heart's desire in Hungary,
spring in my bag
and letters full of the gleaming Danube,
               twittering birds,
the fresh smell of meadows,
and children's letters from Budapest
               to children in Moscow.
Postbag of Paradise.
An envelope is addressed
'Memet,
son of Nâzım Hikmet,
               Turkey.'
In Moscow I'm the one who delivers letters
one by one to their addresses.
But I can't take Memet's letter to his place,
I can't even send it.
Nâzım's son,
the forty thieves have barred the way,
               they won't give him my letter.

May 1954

MY SON IS GROWING UP IN PHOTOGRAPHS

My heart writhes with the pain of a branch whose fruit has been
    plucked,
the image of the road that goes down to the Golden Horn never
    leaves my eyes . . .
a pair of knives stuck right into my heart:
            yearning for my child nostalgia for Istanbul.

Is it impossible to endure separation?
Does our own fate strike us as terrifying?
Do we envy everybody else?
Everyone else's father is in prison in Istanbul,
they want to hang everyone else's son
            in the middle of the road
            in broad daylight.
As for me, here, I am free like the wind
            like a folk song.
You are there, my child,
but you are still too young to be hanged.
People there are willing to risk the gallows
so that everyone else's son won't be hanged
so that everyone else's father won't die
            and bring home a loaf of bread and a kite.
People,
good people,
call out from the four corners of the world,
say stop it,
            don't let the executioner tighten the rope.

1954

'TO CHOP DOWN THE PLANE TREE'

To chop down the plane tree
                their axe strikes at the root,
to set fire to the house
                they stuff oily rags at its base.
The eagle no longer flies
                if its wing is broken,
are we able to think
                if we're hit on the head?

These are the roots of the country;
The sap rising to the branches
            is hidden in the roots,
The founders of hope,
the wings of freedom,
            the wisdom of the people.

So often, in so many places, the root was axed,
the sap failed to rise,
the branches withered,
the wing was broken,
wisdom was killed,
the people driven to the slaughterhouse.

This
is one of the truths of our time.

1956

NEW YEAR'S DAY

Snow fell, all night it fell
lit by the stars.
There is a city, street, a house,
a timber house, far far away.

A child lies on a mattress,
my boy, plump and fair.
No guests, there's no one there
but, through the window, poor Istanbul.

Shrill rang the whistles.
Loneliness is like a prison.
Münevver closed her book
and suddenly, quietly wept.

There is a city, street, a house,
a timber house, far far away.
Snow fell, all night it fell
lit by the stars.

23 March 1956
Moscow, Peredelkino

MÜNEVVER'S LETTER FROM ISTANBUL

Dear love,
I'm writing lying down,
very tired,
I saw my face in the mirror, almost green.
The weather's cold, no sign of summer.
We need thirty lira's worth of wood a week,
                              it's not easy to cope.
Working in the hall just now
I huddled under my blanket.
The windows and window-frames are broken,
the doors don't shut.
It's no longer possible to shelter here,
                    we must move.
The house will collapse on our heads.
To rent would be terribly dear.
Why do I tell you this?
You'll only worry.
But to whom can I pour out my heart?
Forgive me.

If only it would warm up around here,
                         especially at night.
I'm so tired of feeling cold.
In my dreams I go to Africa.
In one I'm in Algiers.
It was hot.
A bullet pierced my forehead.
All my blood streamed away,
                    but I did not die.

Something has happened to me,
I feel I've aged a lot,
– but you know
                I'm not yet forty –
I feel I've aged,

I say so,
But when I do they're angry,
                    they lecture me.
But anyway, enough of this.

Chekhov's 'Grasshopper' has become a film.
It was shown in Paris. They liked it.
Was it all the fault of that poor flighty woman?
I like the doctor
                    but can't forgive the fool.
Who is more unhappy in the end?
                    Who, for whose sake?

The radio played Paraguayan folksongs,
dangerous,
composed with love, sunshine and human sweat,
hopeful and sad.
I have a passion for Paraguayan songs.

I had a letter from Adviye,
she longs to see me,
she can't forget me, it seems . . .
I was surprised.
For years, since you fled your country,
she has never knocked on my door,
                    nor sent any word,
but we met in the street
one festival morning,
she turned her head away and passed.
We were the closest of friends.
But friendship is like a tree,
if it withers
                    it won't turn green again.
I didn't write back.
What's the use?
Even if she comes to my house now
I've nothing to say.
But I'm not at all hostile.

I hope she'll be happy.
She found a rich husband.
But there was something wrong with the man,
      he wasn't right in the head
and Adviye was so full of life.

I've just been to look at our son,
rosy, chestnut-haired, sound asleep.
His quilt had slipped. I covered him up.

There was bad news on the radio this evening;
Irène Joliot Curie has died.
She was still a young woman.

It must have been years ago
I read a book
about the dead one's mother.
Somewhere it talked of her two girl children
– I see the lines now –
like two blonde Greek statues, it said.
Well, one of those children has died.
I don't know how to describe her,
a very clever human being, a great one,
and now the one dead of leukaemia
is her blonde daughter.
I'm very moved by this death.
I cried tonight for Irène Joliot Curie.
How strange.
Irène, they will say, Irène,
      when you died,
          they'll say,
an Istanbul woman
you never knew
would be shocked
and would cry
      for you.
I thought of her husband,
I thought I should write a letter
of sympathy,

but I don't know his address.
If I write Frédéric Joliot Curie, Paris,
                will it reach him?

I read in the paper
A French writer has also died.
Perhaps you've not even heard of him.
He was very old,
an egoist to boot,
                a cynical
                disgusting fellow.
All his life he jeered at everything,
he liked nothing, no one,
just cats and dogs
and only his own.
A few days before he died he gave an interview,
seeming to make a joke of his death
but it was clear he was terrified.
There's a photograph too;
think of grandmother as a man,
put a cap on her head,
                and you've got him!
A puny old man who lived
                with a terrible loneliness.
I was sorry for him too.
Perhaps for his likeness to grandmother,
                perhaps for his loneliness.
I was sorry
but it's certainly not the same pity
you feel about Irène Curie,
when you think of her children, her husband,
you're far sorrier for the world
                which has lost a great human being.

I have good news for you;
your lazy boy is learning to read,
the rascal's had a breakthrough;
'Catch', 'Run', 'Book', 'Pen', 'Bag' . . .
Wonderful, isn't it?

He compares every letter to something:
A is a house,
    B a fat man,
        T is an axe.
I'm scared he'll be lazy.
I'm always wanting him to work.
If he'd been a girl, it would be easy.
All their lives women can tackle any work.
But a boy of five
    how can he manage?
Ah, if only the weather would warm up . . .
It will.
My letter gets longer and longer.
Look after yourself,
answer me soon,
don't forget me,
write to me soon.
And comfort yourself that whatever happens,
Münevver is smart.
I am wretched without you.
Don't forget me,
take good care of yourself.
I kiss you, my love.
Goodnight,
take care.
Write to me soon.
Don't worry about me,
    and don't,
        oh don't, forget me . . .

1956

THE JAPANESE FISHERMAN

A young Japanese fisherman
was killed by a cloud at sea.
I heard this song from his friends,
one lurid yellow evening on the Pacific.

Those who eat the fish we caught, die.
Those who touch our hands, die,
This ship is a black coffin,
you'll die if you come up the gangplank.

Those who eat the fish we caught, die,
not straight away, but slowly,
slowly their flesh rots, falls off.
Those who eat the fish we caught, die.

Those who touch our hands, die.
Our loyal, hardworking hands
washed by salt and sun.
Those who touch our hands, die,
not straight away, but slowly,
slowly their flesh rots, falls off.
Those who touch our hands, die.

Almond Eyes, forget me.
This ship is a black coffin,
you'll die if you come up the gangplank.
The cloud has passed over us.

Almond Eyes, forget me.
Don't hug me my darling,
you'll catch death from me.
Almond Eyes, forget me.

This ship is a black coffin.
Almond Eyes, forget me
The child you have from me
will be rotten from a rotten egg.
This ship is a black coffin.
This sea is a dead sea.
Human beings, where are you?
                    Where are you?

1956

'LIGHT OF MY EYE, MY DARLING!'

My Mansur of Port Said, aged thirteen or fourteen years,
barefoot, head close-cropped, sits shining shoes
by his box with its mirrors and bells.
High heels, soft shoes, army boots, walking shoes,
dusty, muddy, hopeless,
worn out, old,
mount the box with its mirrors.
Brushes take wing, red velvet glows,
high heels, soft shoes, army boots, walking shoes,
joyous, lively, young,
hopeful, shining,
step off the box with its mirrors.

My Mansur, dark and skinny
like a date-stone,
my sweet Mansur
always sings the same song:
'light of my eye, my darling!' . . .

They set fire to Port Said, they killed Mansur:
I saw his photograph this morning in the paper;
a little corpse among corpses.
'Light of my eye, my darling!'
like a date-stone.

26 *November* 1956
Prague

I GOT A LETTER FROM MÜNEVVER, SHE SAYS:

Tell me, Nâzım, about the city where I was born.
I understand I was very little when I left Sofia,
but I could speak Bulgarian . . .
What sort of a city is Sofia?
My mother used to tell me
that Sofia was minuscule.
It must have grown:
just think,
it's been forty-one years.
There used to be a 'Boris Park':
I understand my governess took me there mornings.
That's probably the biggest park in Sofia.
I still have snapshots of me taken there:
a park with lots of sun and shade.
Go, sit there.
Maybe, by chance, you'll sit on the bench I played around.
But, then, benches wouldn't last forty years, would they?
They must have rotted and been replaced.
Trees are best of all,
they live longer than our memories of them . . .
Go, sit there one day under the oldest chestnut.
Forget everything,
even our separation,
think of me, only me.

11 *June* 1957
Varna

I WROTE A LETTER TO MÜNEVVER, I SAID:

The trees are standing, but the old benches are dead,
'Boris Park' is now 'Freedom Park',
under the chestnut I thought only of you,
only of you, that means Memet too
only you and Memet, that means my country . . .

11 *June* 1957
Varna

THE WALNUT TREE

My head is a foaming cloud, inside and outside I'm the sea.
I am a walnut tree in Gülhane Park in Istanbul,
an old walnut tree with knots and scars.
You don't know this and the police don't either.

I am a walnut tree in Gülhane Park.
My leaves sparkle like fish in water,
my leaves flutter like silk handkerchiefs.
Break one off, my darling, and wipe your tears.
My leaves are my hands – I have a hundred thousand hands.
Istanbul I touch you with a hundred thousand hands.
My leaves are my eyes, and I am shocked at what I see.
I look at you, Istanbul, with a hundred thousand eyes
and my leaves beat, beat with a hundred thousand hearts.

I am a walnut tree in Gülhane Park.
You don't know this and the police don't either.

1 *July* 1957
Balçık

THE LAST BUS

Midnight, the last bus,
the conductor has punched the ticket.
There's no bad news waiting for me at home,
                    nor a rakı-feast either.
What waits for me is the Great Divide.
I walk to it fearless,
                    untroubled.

The great darkness is closing in.
Now I can watch the world,
                    relaxed and calm.
A friend's treachery no longer upsets me
            or the knife-thrust as he shakes my hand.
The enemy provokes me now in vain.
I passed through the forest of idols
                    mowing them down,
                    they were not easy to overturn.
I put my beliefs to the test again,
            they were mostly untainted, thank God.
But my condition wasn't so brilliant
                    nor so free as now.

The great darkness is closing in.
Now I can watch the world,
                    relaxed and calm.
I look up from work,
suddenly from the past appears
                              a word
                              a smell
                              a gesture.
A friendly word
            a good smell
                    my lover's hand in mine.
Recalling memories no longer saddens me.
I don't mind memories.

I've no complaints,
not even of the heartache
that like an aching tooth never stops;

The great darkness is closing in.
No more disdainful ministers or fawning clerks.
Dousing myself from head to foot in light
I can look at the sun without blinking.
And perhaps – what a shame! –
                even the cleverest lie
                        deceives me no longer.
No words intoxicate me now,
my own or any other's.

And now, my darling,
death is very near.
The world is a world more beautiful than ever.
I was clothed with the world,
                I've started to strip.
I was at the train window
                now I've arrived at the station.
I was inside the house
                now I'm at the door with no lock.
I love guests even more.
Heat is more golden than ever before,
                snow more pure.

21 July 1957
Prague

OPTIMISM

I write poems,
they don't get published
but they will get published.

I wait for a letter to bring me good news
maybe it will come on the day I die
but it will come.

No state nor money
the world will be run by human beings
maybe it will happen a hundred years from now
no matter

but this is the way it's going to happen for sure.

12 *September* 1957
Moscow

A JOURNEY

We open doors,
we close doors,
we pass through doors,
and at the end of the one and only journey
                              there's no city,
                                   no harbour;
the train comes off the rails,
the boat sinks,
the plane crashes.
The map is drawn on ice.
But if I could choose to set out or not
                              on this journey
                                   I'd do it again.

Leningrad
1958

STRONTIUM 90

We are having very strange weather,
sun, rain, snow.
They say it's as a result of the nuclear tests.

It's been raining Strontium 90
      on the grass, the milk, the meat,
      on hope, on freedom:
      on the great longing
      whose door we knocked at.

We are in a race against each other, my darling.
Either we'll take life to the dead stars,
or death will descend on our world.

6 *March* 1958
Warsaw

FABLE OF FABLES

We are by the waterside
the plane tree and I.
Our reflections are thrown on the water
the plane tree's and mine.
The sparkle of the water hits us
the plane tree and me.

We are by the waterside
the plane tree, I and the cat.
Our reflections are thrown on the water
the plane tree's, mine and the cat's.
The sparkle of the water hits us
the plane tree, me and the cat.

We are by the waterside
the plane tree, I, the cat and the sun.
Our reflections are thrown on the water
the plane tree's, mine, the cat's and the sun's.
The sparkle of the water hits us
the plane tree, me, the cat and the sun.

We are by the waterside
the plane tree, I, the cat, the sun and our life.
Our reflections are thrown on the water
the plane tree's, mine, the cat's, the sun's and our life's.
The sparkle of the water hits us
the plane tree, me, the cat, the sun and our life.

We are by the waterside.
First the cat will go
its reflection will be lost on the water.
Then I will go
my reflection will be lost on the water.
Then the plane tree will go
its reflection will be lost on the water.

Then the water will go
the sun will remain
then it will go too.

We are by the waterside
the plane tree, I, the cat, the sun and our life.
The water is cool
the plane tree is huge
I am writing a poem
the cat is dozing
the sun is warm
it's good to be alive.
The sparkle of the water hits us
the plane tree, me, the cat, the sun, our life.

7 March 1958
Warsaw

CHATTING WITH NEZVAL WHO DIED

As soon as you'd gone
the weather turned cold, it snowed.
The sky, they said,
was shedding tears for the dying.
But you know on the thirteenth of April
spring broke.
Prague burst into smiles
even in the graveyard.
They talk about you still
a little solemnly like praying.
In the window
where your photograph is draped in black
it's sunny, bright.
The weather can still turn bad
though May lies ahead.
In Prague, you know, when May,
fresh green, golden yellow,
assails the streets,
young girls wipe away grief
like cleaning window-panes,
and the sorrow for you that remains
will be lost like your shadow
from Prague's pavements.
It's the way of the world . . . but in fact
the kind-hearted dead, the wise ones,
life-lovers,
don't wish 41 days of mourning
or say 'Après moi le Déluge!'
They depart leaving
some useful objects, a word,
a tree, a smile;
they bear alone
what they can't share with the living,
the darkness of the grave
and the weight of their stone.

Since they asked nothing from the living
they seem not to have died . . .
Nezval, I know that you,
you too are like that,
one of Prague's dead,
kind-hearted, wise, loving the world . . .

They phoned – alas,
now you're gone from our sight.
Nezval, my friend, take care!
In our world
the sweetest fruit is still the light . . .

20 *April* 1958
Prague

BEES

Bees like big drops of honey,
bees carrying vines to the sun,
came flying out of my youth;
these apples too are from there,
       these heavy apples,
this golden-dusty road,
these white pebbles along the stream,
my belief in folksong,
my lack of envy,
and this cloudless day,
       this blue day
the sea hot, stripped bare, lying back,
this longing,
the gleaming teeth of a full-lipped mouth,
they came out of my youth
to this Caucasian village
like big drops of honey on the feet of bees,
       from somewhere in my forgotten youth,
       from somewhere;
       I never had enough of that somewhere.

13 September 1958
Arkhipo Osipovka

OLD MAN ON THE SHORE

Plunging mountains range upon range
pinewoods descending to the sea
an old rugged man on the shore
stretched out his back on the pebbles

and this sun-ripe September day
with its faraway message of sunk ships
the north-east wind deep blue and cool
was caressing the old man's face

and his hands on his belly
were like two crabs weary and stubborn
tough-skinned pitiless trophies
of a journey stronger than time

his wrinkled eyelids crusty with salt
suddenly gently closed
in this gold-flecked darkness
the old man heard the roaring

the sea and its long-toothed fish
the flaming dawns
the flowers that open on the rocky seabed
fishing-nets and fishermen's cabins

but perhaps it was the roar of pine-tops
near the clouds
he knew how dizzy a man can feel
when he looks at them from below

plunging mountains range upon range
pinewoods descending to the sea
an old rugged man on the shore
stretched out his back on the pebbles

24 September 1958   *Pitsun*

GREAT HUMANITY

Great humanity sails on ships as deck passengers
   rides trains third-class
   travels highways on foot
Great humanity goes to work at the age of eight
   marries at twenty
   dies at forty:
   great humanity.
There is enough bread for everyone except great humanity
   rice too
   same with sugar
   and cloth
   books as well
   there is enough of them for all except great humanity.
There is no shadow on the ground of great humanity
   no lamps in its streets
   no pane in its windows
But great humanity has its hopes
   there can be no life without hope.

7 October 1958
Tashkent

THE OPTIMIST

He never tore wings off flies when he was little,
or tied cans to cats' tails,
or kept cockroaches in matchboxes,
he didn't destroy ants' nests.
When he grew up
they did all that to him.
I was by his deathbed.
'Read me a poem,' he said,
'about the sun, the sea,
about atomic reactors and satellites,
about mankind's great achievements.'

6 December 1958
Baku

THE ICEBREAKER

The icebreaker in front,
our boat shuddering close behind,
I looked from my cabin porthole,
at the frozen sea, white and rigid!
I am from Istanbul,
I grew up by the hot salty seashore.
We love colour and light and all things clearly alive.
We have poppy fields,
streets,
the covered market,
pigeons,
but most alive is our sea
that blue-green of ours,
more impatient than the north wind,
    more agile than dolphins.
Sometimes on summer afternoons
  when a leaf hardly stirs in the air
    it moves
      vast, boundless,
        flashing, clean.
We never lose its smell.
I looked from my cabin porthole,
at the frozen sea
    rigid
      white.

I looked
  and swore.

1959
Leningrad to Stockholm

TWO LOVES

Two loves can't exist in one heart,
not true –
it happens.

In the city of cold rains
I lie at night in the hotel room
staring up at the ceiling,
where clouds pass
slowly like trucks on wet asphalt;
and far away to the right
            a white building
            perhaps of a hundred storeys,
a golden needle gleaming on its roof.
Clouds cross the ceiling, sunladen clouds like melon-boats.
I sit at the bay window,
waterlight glints on my face,
am I on the shore of a river
            or by the sea?

What's on that tray,
that tray with roses,
wild strawberries or purple mulberries?
Am I in a field of narcissi
or a snowy beech wood?
The women I love are laughing and crying
                        in two tongues.

Friends, how did you come together?
You don't know each other,
Where are you waiting for me?
In the Plane Tree Café at Beyazit or in Gorky Park?

In the city of cold rains
I lie on my back at night in the hotel room
eyes wide open, burning.

Someone played a tune,
begun on a mouth-organ, ending on a lute.
In my heart utter confusion intertwined
with a great longing for two cities far away.

Leap out of bed,
race through the rain,
race to the station.
'Drive, my Engineer friend!
        take me back there.'

'Where?'

17 July 1959

THE THREE STORKS RESTAURANT

We used to meet at the Three Storks Restaurant in Prague.
Now I stand eyes closed by a roadside,
    you a death's distance away.
Perhaps there's no Three Storks Restaurant in Prague
    I'm making it up.

We used to meet at the Three Storks Restaurant in Prague.
I used to look in your face and sing from my heart
    the prophet Solomon's Song of Songs.

We used to meet at the Three Storks Restaurant in Prague.
Now I stand eyes closed by a roadside,
    you a death's distance away,
        in a cracked mirror, awry, deformed.

We used to meet at the Three Storks Restaurant in Prague.
O Sonya Danyolova, dear old friend,
nothing's so soon forgotten as the dead.

18 *August* 1959

MORNING DARKNESS

In the morning darkness telegraph poles,
                              a road.
    In the morning darkness the chest with its shiny mirror,
                              table,
                              slippers,
objects see and know each other again.
    In our room the morning darkness brightens like a sail.
    In our room the blue coolness is like a diamond ring.
The stars grow white in our room.

Very far away
          in the stream bed in the sky the pebbles are bleached.
My rose's head is on the pillow,
          her head is on a really wide feather pillow.
Her hands like two white tulips on the eiderdown.
The birds start singing in her hair.

In the morning darkness the city with its trees and factory
    chimneys.
In the morning darkness the trees are wet, the factory
    chimneys hot.
In the morning darkness caressing the road
                the first footsteps pass our room,
                    first noise of a motor,
                    first laugh,
                        first curse,
the börek-seller's steaming glass box,
the driver in his boots entering the dairy,
the neighbours' crying child,
the dove in Picasso's blue picture,
the mannequin in the window,
          with its yellow shoes,
and the Chinese fans made of sandalwood,
the full, red lips of my darling,

the happiest and freshest of all awakenings
come and go in our room in the morning darkness.

In the morning darkness I turn on the radio,
giant numbers and giant mines with giant names muddled together,
oil wells, maize fields compete with each other.
The shepherd who got the Lenin medal,
(I see his picture on the front pages,
his thick moustache, drooping, black)
speaks like a young girl, shy and bashful.
News comes from the North and South Poles,
then this morning at six o'clock
when Sputnik III
orbits the world 8879 times
the huge eyes of my rose open on the pillow.
They are still like smoky mountain lakes,
blue fish flick through their deep pools,
green pine trees in their depths.
They look deep and straight.
The end of her dreams shimmers in the morning darkness.
I become light,
I see and know myself again,
I am utterly happy,
       I am a bit shy,
          just a bit.

Like a sail ready for the journey,
       like a bright sail,
           darkness in our room in the morning.
My rose comes out of the bed naked as an apricot,
the bed in the morning darkness is white as the dove
              in the blue poster.

February 1960
Kislovodsk

'MY WOMAN CAME WITH ME AS FAR AS BREST'

My woman came with me as far as Brest,
she got off the train and stayed on the platform,
she grew smaller and smaller,
she became a grain of wheat in the endless blue,
then I saw only the rails.

She called from Poland, I couldn't answer.
I couldn't ask, 'Where are you, my love, where are you?'
'Come to me!' she said but I couldn't come;
the train raced on as if it would never stop,
I'm choking with grief.

Pockets of snow were rotting in the sandy earth,
then suddenly I knew my woman could see me.
'Have you forgotten, have you forgotten me?' she was asking
while spring walked the sky on naked muddy feet.

Then stars descended and landed on the telegraph wires
and darkness was beating on the train like rain,
my woman was standing under the telegraph poles,
her heart pounding as if she was in my arms,
the telegraph poles came and went but she never moved,
the train raced on as if it would never stop,
I was choking with grief.

Then suddenly I realized I'd been living on this train for
    long, long years
– I'm still surprised by how I knew –
always singing the same great hopeful song,
always receding from the women and cities I loved,
carrying longings like a wound in my flesh,
and getting nearer to somewhere, to somewhere.

March 1960
The Mediterranean

IN BEYAZIT SQUARE

A dead man lies,
  a youth of nineteen years,
  in the sun by day,
  under the stars by night,
  in Istanbul, in Beyazıt Square.

A dead man lies,
  in one hand a notebook,
  in one hand his dream gone
  before it began, in April 1960,
  in Istanbul, in Beyazıt Square.

A dead man lies
  shot,
  a bullet-wound
  like a red carnation open on his forehead,
  in Istanbul, in Beyazıt Square.

A dead man will lie,
  his blood seeping into the earth,
  until my country comes with arms and freedom songs
      and takes
         the great square
           by force.

May 1960

FLAXEN HAIR

To Vera Tulyakova with deep respect

The express entered the station at dawn unannounced.
It was covered in snow.
I was on the platform with my coat collar up.
On the platform there was no one but me.
One of the sleeping car windows stopped right in front of me.
The curtain was half open.
A young woman was sleeping on the lower bunk in the twilight,
flaxen-haired, her eyelashes blue,
and her full red lips sulky and pouting.
I couldn't see who was sleeping on the upper bunk.
The express glided out of the station unannounced.
I don't know where it came from or where it was going.
I watched it go.
Now I am the sleeper in the upper bunk.
I hadn't been in such deep sleep for years,
even in the Bristol Hotel in Warsaw
although my bed was wooden and narrow.
A young woman is sleeping in another bed,
flaxen-haired, her eyelashes blue,
her white neck long and curved,
she hadn't been in such deep sleep for years,
even though her bed was wooden and narrow.
Time was advancing quickly. We were approaching midnight.
We hadn't been in such deep sleep for years,
even though the beds were wooden and narrow.
I am going downstairs from the fourth floor –
the lift is still broken.
I am going downstairs in the mirrors.
Maybe I'm twenty, maybe I'm a hundred years old.
Time was advancing quickly. We were approaching midnight.
On the third floor a woman is laughing behind a door,
in my right hand a sorrowful rose slowly opens.
On the second floor by the snowy windows I met a ballerina
    from Cuba.
She passed through my mind like a fresh dark flame.

The poet Nicholas Guillen returned to Havana a long time ago.
For years he had spent his life sitting
in the lobbies of European and Asian hotels.
We drank the longing for our cities drop by drop.
There are two things that are forgotten only in death:
the face of our mother and the face of our city.
The doorman wished me a safe journey,
his sheepskin submerged in night.
I walked in the freezing wind and the neon lights.
Time was advancing quickly. I was approaching midnight.
Suddenly they appeared before me.
It was light there like day
there was no one to see them but me.
They were a squad. They had short boots, trousers, jackets,
on their sleeves this swastika sign.
In their hands they had automatics.
They had shoulders and helmets but no heads,
between shoulders and helmets there was a void,
they even had collars and necks but no heads.
Among them were soldiers for whose death no one cried.
We walked on:
it was clear they were frightened, afraid with an animal fear.
I cannot say it was clear from their eyes –
no heads meant no eyes.
It was clear they were frightened, afraid with an animal fear.
It was clear from their boots.
Can fear be seen from boots?
Theirs was, because of their fear they began to shoot without
        stopping
at all buildings, all vehicles, all living creatures.
They shot at every noise, every tiny movement.
They even shot at a poster of blue fish in Chopin Street,
but not a piece of plaster falls, not a window breaks
and there is no one but me to hear the sounds of the bullets.
Even though the dead are an SS squad, dead people can't kill,
the dead only kill when they live again, a worm boring into
        an apple
but it was clear they were frightened, afraid with an animal fear.
Hadn't this city been murdered before they were murdered?

Hadn't this city's bones been broken one by one,
and its skin flayed?
Wasn't a book cover made from its skin,
soap from its fat, string from its hair?
But here it was standing against them in the night and freezing
    wind
like a hot baguette.
Time was advancing quickly. I was approaching midnight.
On the way to the Belvedere I thought about the Poles
playing a heroic mazurka throughout their history.
On the way to the Belvedere I thought about the Poles.
They gave me my first, maybe my last, decoration in this palace.
The master of ceremonies opened the gilded white door
and I entered the great hall with a young woman,
flaxen-haired, her eyelashes blue.
There was no one around but the two of us
and the water colours and tiny chairs, sofas
like in a dolls' house, and because of that
you were a painting in light blue.
Maybe you were a doll,
maybe you were a flashback from my dream dropped on my
    left breast,
in the twilight on the lower bunk.
Your white neck was long and curved.
You hadn't been in such deep sleep for years,
and here is the Caprice Bar in Cracow.
Time is advancing quickly. We are approaching midnight.
On the table between your coffee cup and my lemonade was
    separation.
You put it there. It was water down a stone well.
I lean and look.
An old man smiles indistinctly at a cloud.
I am calling. I lost you – echoes of my voice come back.
Separation was on the table in the packet of cigarettes.
A waiter in glasses brought it – you ordered it.
Curling smoke in your eyes from the tip of your cigarette
and in your palm which was ready to say goodbye.
Separation on the table just where your elbow was leaning.
Separation was passing through your mind,

in what you hid and did not hide from me.
Separation was in your ease, in your trust in me.
Separation was in your great fear,
suddenly falling in love is like a sudden opening of your door.
You love me but are unaware.
Separation was in your unawareness.
Separation was freed from gravity.
It had no weight, I can't say it was like a feather –
even a feather has weight, separation has no weight,
but there it was.
Time is advancing quickly. Midnight approaches.
We walked in the darkness of the mediaeval walls touching the stars.
Time was flowing quickly backwards;
the echoes of our footsteps sounded like yellow scrawny dogs
running ahead of us.
The devil wanders in Yegelon University sinking his nails in
        the rocks,
trying to break Copernicus' astrolabes that date from the Arabs,
and dancing rock and roll with the Catholic students in the
        marketplace
under the arches of the cloth merchants' bazaar.
Time is advancing quickly. We are approaching midnight.
The glow of Nova Huta is reflected in the clouds,
then the young workers from the villages pour out their souls
        with the metal
flaming into new moulds and the pouring of souls
is a thousand times more difficult than the pouring of metal.
The trumpet playing the hours in the bell tower of the church
of the Virgin Mary sounded midnight.
Its cry from the middle ages rose
and announced that the enemy was approaching the city.
It went quiet when the arrow suddenly pierced its throat.
The trumpet died in peace,
and I thought about the pain of seeing the enemy approach
and being killed unable to raise the alarm.
Time is advancing quickly. Midnight is left behind
like a harbour whose lights have gone out.
The express entered the station at dawn unannounced.
Prague was all in rain.

It was a chest inlaid with silver at the bottom of a lake.
I opened its lid:
inside a young woman sleeps among glass birds,
flaxen-haired, her eyelashes blue.
For years she hadn't been in such deep sleep.
I closed the lid and loaded the chest on the freight car.
The express glided out of the station, unannounced.
I looked behind, arms hanging at my sides.
Prague was all in rain.
There is no you.
You're sleeping in the lower bunk in the twilight.
The upper bunk is empty.
There is no you.
One of the most beautiful cities in the world is emptied,
like a glove from which you have taken your hand,
now its lights went off like mirrors that cannot see you.
The Vltava water flows under the bridges like lost evenings.
The streets are empty,
curtains are drawn in all the windows.
Trams pass by empty,
no drivers even or ticket collectors.
Cafés are empty,
so are the restaurants and bars.
Shop windows are empty:
no cloth, no crystal, no meat, no wine,
not a book, not a packet of sweets,
not a carnation.
In this loneliness which surrounds the whole city like mist
an old person,
to shake off the cares of age increased tenfold by loneliness,
throws bread to sea gulls from the Legionnaire's bridge,
        soaking each crumb
in his young heart's blood.
I want to catch time,
the gold dust of its speed
remains in my fingers.
In the wagon-lit a woman sleeps in the lower bunk.
For years she hadn't been in such deep sleep,
flaxen-haired, her eyelashes blue.

Her hands were candles in silver candlesticks.
I couldn't see who was sleeping in the upper bunk.
If there is somebody sleeping there, it's not me.
Maybe the upper bunk is empty,
perhaps it was Moscow in the upper bunk.
Fog has fallen on the Polish land
as it fell on Brest.
For two days planes cannot land or take off,
but trains come and go through the pupils of weeping eyes.
From Berlin I was by myself in the compartment.
I woke up next morning to sun on snowy plains.
In the restaurant car I drank a kind of ayran called kefir.
The waitress recognized me:
she had seen two of my plays in Moscow.
A young woman met me at the station,
her waist was as slim as an ant's,
flaxen-haired, her eyelashes blue.
I held her hand as we walked.
We walked in the sun, crunching snow underfoot.
That year spring had come early.
Those were the days we flew messages to Venus.
Moscow was happy, I was happy, we were happy.
I lost you suddenly in Mayakovsky Square. Suddenly I lost you,
but it wasn't sudden because first I lost the warmth of your hand
    in my palm,
then I lost your hand's soft weight in my palm, then your hand,
and the separation had already begun long ago in the first touch
    of our fingers,
and still I lost you suddenly.
In the asphalt seas I stopped cars, looked in them – you were
    not there.
The boulevards were snowy,
amongst the footprints none of yours.
I can recognize your footprints at once with boots, shoes,
    stockings, barefoot.
I asked the police
haven't you seen her? . . .
Impossible not to notice her hands if she took off her gloves . . .
Her hands like candles in silver candlesticks.

The police answered very politely:
we haven't seen her.
In Istanbul a tugboat struggles against the Sarayburnu current,
three barges behind it.
Sea gulls squawk and scream.
From Red Square I shouted to the barges. I couldn't shout
        to the Captain
of the tug because the engine was roaring
so he couldn't hear my voice and the captain was tired
and his jacket buttons were torn off.
From Red Square I shouted to the barges.
We haven't seen her.
I keep joining all the queues in all the streets of Moscow
and ask only women,
woollen-scarved, smiling faces, patient, silent old women,
and rosy-cheeked, curved-nosed, young beauties in green
        velvet hats,
and young girls, pure as snow, tight-clothed and really chic.
Maybe they are terrible old hags, depressed and silly
        young girls,
but I don't care.
A woman sees beauty before men do and never forgets it.
Haven't you seen her?
Flaxen-haired, her eyelashes blue,
a black coat with a white collar and huge mother-of-pearl buttons.
She bought it in Prague.
We haven't seen her.
I am racing with time, it overtakes, then I do.
I am scared I can't see
its diminishing red lights when it overtakes me.
When I'm ahead its headlights cast my shadow on the street.
My shadow runs, I'm alarmed
that I'm going to lose sight of my shadow before me.
I try theatres, concerts, cinemas
but not the Bolshoi – you don't like the opera that's on tonight.
I went into the Fisherman's Tavern at Kalamış and I talked
        like old friends with Sait Faik.
A month ago I came out of prison. He had pains in his liver.
        The world was wonderful.

I go into restaurants, there are orchestras, jazz bands with famous
    players,
silver-embroidered tip-loving doormen and distracted waiters,
I ask the cloakroom attendants and our local watchman:
we haven't seen her.
Midnight struck from the Strastnoy Monastery clock tower,
though the monastery and clock tower were destroyed long ago.
They're making the biggest cinema in the city there.
There I met my nineteen years.
We recognized each other at once,
although we hadn't even seen each others' faces in photographs,
yet we recognized each other at once. We were not surprised, we
    wanted to shake hands,
but our hands can't touch. Between us stand forty years
an endless frozen Northern sea,
and on Strastnoy Square – now Pushkin Square – snow began
    to fall.
I am cold, especially my hands and feet,
though I've got woollen socks, shoes and fur gloves.
It was he who was without socks, with bare hands,
and feet wrapped in cloth inside his boots,
in his mouth the world had the taste of an unripe apple,
his palms had the firmness
of a fourteen-year-old girl's breast.
In his eyes songs stretched for miles, death a puny inch,
and he was totally unaware of anything that would befall him,
only I know what he has to face
because I believed in everything he believed.
I loved all the women he would love.
I've written all the poems he would write.
I've done every stretch he would do.
I've passed through all the cities he would pass.
I've suffered every illness he would suffer.
I've slept every sleep and dreamed every dream he would dream.
I've lost everything he would lose.
Flaxen-haired, her eyelashes blue,
a black coat with a white collar and huge mother-of-pearl buttons.
I haven't seen her.

II

My nineteen years cross Beyazit Square and go up to Red
    Square,
go down to the Concorde where I meet Abidin and we talk
    about squares.
The day before Gagarin returned from going round the
    biggest square.
Titov will go round and return and he'll do it seventeen and
    a half
times but I don't know about that yet.
We talk about squares and buildings with Abidin in my attic
    hotel room.
The river Seine flows on both sides of Notre Dame.
At night from my window I see the river Seine like a slice
of moon in the harbour of stars
and a young woman sleeps in my attic room
which mingles with the chimneys of Paris roofs . . .
She hasn't been in such deep sleep for years,
flaxen-haired, curved eyelashes blue are a cloud on her face.
We talk to Abidin about the seeds of squares and the seeds
    of buildings.
We talk about Jelaleddin Rumi whirling in the square.
Abidin pours out the endless speed of colours.
I eat colours like fruit
and Matisse is a fruit seller and sells cosmic fruit –
our Abidin and Avni and Levni do the same.
The buildings, the squares, the colours
seen by the microscope and lens of the rocket,
their poets and painters and musicians;
Abidin paints their progress in a space
of 150 by 60.
Seeing the fish in the water
and catching the fish in the water
I can see and catch time as it flows restless in Abidin's canvas,
and the Seine is like a slice of moon,
and a young woman is sleeping on a moon slice.
How many times have I lost her and found her, how many times
and how many times again will I lose her and find her.

That's it, that's it my girl, I threw part of my life
into the Seine from St Michel bridge.
Monsieur Dupont will catch a part of my life on his fishing line
one drizzly morning daybreak.
Monsieur Dupont will pull it out of the waters
with the blue image of Paris and a part of my life will be
like nothing, neither a fish nor an old boot.
Monsieur Dupont will throw it back together with the image
  of Paris
and the image will stay in the old place.
A part of my life will flow with the river Seine
to the great cemetery of rivers.
I woke with a rustle of blood flowing in my veins.
My fingers are weightless,
my fingers and toes cut off from my hands and feet
will float on the air and turn gently hovering above my head.
I've got no right, no left, no up, no down.
Better tell Abidin he should paint the fallen hero
in Beyazit Square and comrade Gagarin and comrade Titov,
whose name and fame I don't know yet or his appearance
  or the ones after him
or the young woman lying in the attic.
I returned from Cuba this morning. In Cuba Square six million
  people,
white, black, yellow, mixed, plant a bright seed,
the seed of seeds in joy and happiness.
Can you paint a picture of happiness, Abidin,
not taking the easy way out?
Not the picture of an angel-faced mother who suckles her
  rosy-cheeked baby,
nor of apples on a white tablecloth,
nor goldfish swimming around among bubbles in the aquarium.
Can you paint a picture of happiness, Abidin?
Can you paint the picture of Cuba in the height of summer 1961?
of 'Thank goodness, thank goodness,' Mister painter, 'I have
  seen this day.
Now if I die, I won't give a damn.'
Can you paint the picture of 'What a pity to be born in Havana
  this morning'?

I saw a hand 150 kilometres east of Havana close to the
seashore.
I saw a hand on a wall.
The wall was a happy song.
The hand was stroking the wall.
The hand was six months old stroking the neck of his mother.
The hand was seventeen years old and was stroking the breast
of Maria.
Its palm was callused and smelt of the Caribbean,
twenty years old and the hand was stroking the neck of his
six-month-old son.
The hand was twenty-five years old and has long forgotten
how to stroke.
The hand was thirty years old and I've seen it.
I have seen it on a wall by the seashore 150 kilometres east
of Havana.
It was stroking the wall. You who paint hands, Abidin,
paint, Abidin, the picture of the hand of our blacksmiths,
draw the hand of the Cuban fisherman in charcoal,
the hand of the Cuban fisherman Nicholas, who will never
again forget
how to stroke the wall of his gleaming house,
which he got from the cooperative,
a huge hand,
a sea-turtle hand,
a hand that doesn't believe it can stroke a happy wall,
a hand finally believing in every happiness,
a sunny seaside sacred hand,
the hand of hopes which sprout and grow green and become
honeyed
with the speed of sugar cane on the fertile lands
like the words of Fidel.
One of the hands planting houses like many-coloured cool trees
and trees like comfortable houses in Cuba in 1961.
One of the hands that got ready to pour steel.
They turn machine guns into songs and songs into machine
guns,
the hand of freedom without lies,
the hand that Fidel shook,

the hand that writes the little word freedom with life's first pencil
on the first page of life.
When they say the word freedom the Cubans' mouths water
as if they were cutting open a honeydew melon,
and the mens' eyes sparkle.
The girls' hearts throb when their lips touch the word freedom.
The old ones pull their sweet memories from the well,
drinking them in draughts.
Can you paint the picture of happiness, Abidin,
the picture of the word freedom, the word without lies?
It is evening in Paris.
Notre Dame turns on and off like an orange light,
and in Paris all the old and new stones went on and off like
    an orange lamp.
I think about our crafts, those of poetry, painting, music
and others. I think and I understand
that a huge river has flowed ever since the hand of man drew
the first bison in the first cave
and then all the streams with new fish,
new water weeds, new tastes mingling,
and it is the only one which flows endless, boundless
and never dries up.
In Paris there should be a chestnut tree,
the first chestnut of Paris, the ancestor of all Paris chestnuts,
it came from Istanbul and settled in Paris from the Bosphorus slopes.
I don't know whether it's still alive – if it's alive it should be
about two hundred years old. I would like to go and kiss its hand,
I would like us to go and lie in its shadow with those who make
the paper of this book, who typeset the text, who print it
    and lay it out,
and those who sell this book in the shops, those who pay money
    to buy it
and who buy and look at it, and then there are Abidin and me and
    that woman
with the flaxen hair who makes my head and heart ache.

Train: Warsaw, Krakov, Prague,
Moscow, Paris, Havana, Moscow

'MY TIME IS COMING'

My time is coming
when I'll suddenly leap into emptiness.
I'll never know of my decaying flesh
or the maggots crawling in my eye sockets.

I think of death non-stop
which means my time is near.

10 *September* 1961
Leipzig

AUTOBIOGRAPHY

I was born in 1902
I never went back to the town where I was born
I don't like to go back
When I was 3 my grandfather was a Pasha in Aleppo
At 19 I was a student at the Communist University in Moscow
At 49 I was in Moscow again invited by the Central Committee
I have been writing poetry since I was 14

Some people are experts on plants, some on fish –
                         I am an expert on partings
Some people know the names of the stars by heart
                         I know longings

I have slept in prisons and big hotels
I have been hungry and on hunger strike in prison and tasted
    almost every food

When I was 30 they wanted to hang me
At 48 they wanted to give me the Peace Medal
                         – and did
At 36 I spent half a year pacing a four metre square concrete cell
At 59 I flew from Prague to Havana in 18 hours

I never saw Lenin, but I took part in a vigil at his coffin in 1924
and in 1961 I visited him in the mausoleum of his books

They tried in vain to snatch me from my party
I was not crushed under the falling idols
In 1951 with a young friend on the Black Sea I headed for death
In 1952 I waited to die, on my back for 4 months with a damaged
    heart

I was desperately jealous of the women I loved
but I was never envious of anyone even Chaplin
I deceived my women
I did not talk behind my friends' backs

I drank, but was not a drunkard
I was so happy that I could eke out my living by hard work
        and sweat

If I felt shame for someone I lied
I lied so as not to grieve others
        but I also lied for no reason

I rode in trains, planes, cars –
most people cannot
I went to the opera
        – most people haven't been there or even heard of it
From the age of 21 I haven't been to where most people go –
        not to mosque, church, temple, synagogue, or sorcerers –
        but I have had my coffee grounds read

My books are published in 30 or 40 languages
but in my own Turkish, in my own Turkey
        I am banned

I haven't got cancer yet
there's no law that says I will
I'll never be Prime Minister or anything like that
quite honestly I'm not interested anyway
Also I never fought in the war
or went down into the shelters at midnight
I didn't throw myself down on the road when the planes
        dived –
but I fell passionately in love when I was sixty

To cut a long story short, comrades,
even if I'm dying of grief today in Berlin
        I can say 'I have lived like a decent man'
and who knows how much longer
        I'll live and what more will happen to me?

11 *September* 1961
This autobiography was written in East Berlin

'FROM STONE, BRONZE, PLASTER, PAPER'

From stone, bronze, plaster, paper
from two centimetres to seven metres
in all the city squares we were under his boots
of stone, bronze, plaster, paper
and his shadow of stone, bronze, plaster, paper
hung over our park trees
His moustache of stone, bronze, plaster, paper
was in our soup in the restaurants
In our rooms we were under his eyes
of stone, bronze, plaster, paper
Then one morning they disappeared
His boots disappeared from the squares
His shadow no longer hung over our trees
His moustache was no longer in our soup
His eyes departed from our rooms
and the pressure of thousands of tons
of stone, bronze, plaster, paper
was lifted off our chests.

13 *December* 1961
Moscow

WHERE HAVE WE COME FROM,
WHERE ARE WE GOING?

The beginning

Since we first stood upright on two feet,
since we first stretched an arm a club's length,
       since we first cut stone,
              we became makers and destroyers,
makers and destroyers are what we are, my love,
       in this world to be lived in.

On the ways behind us our footsteps are printed in blood,
on the ways behind us our high aspirations of hand and mind
       and heart
are present in clay, stone or bronze, on canvas, in steel and
       plastic.

Will our footprints continue bloody on the ways ahead?
Will our ways ahead finish in hell's blind alley?

  *   *   *   *   *

The call

God is our hands,
God is our hearts and minds.
God who is everywhere present,
in earth, in stone, in bronze, on canvas, in steel and plastic,
in the numbers and lines of the singer's high harmonies.

I call on you, human beings;
on behalf of books and trees and fish,
of the grain of wheat, of rice and of sundrenched streets,
of grape-black hair, wheat-blonde hair and children.

Our days wait their turn in the hands of children,
our days are seeds in the hands of children,
in the hands of children they will grow green.

22 November 1962

MY FUNERAL

Will my funeral start in our courtyard below?
How will you bring my coffin down three floors?
The lift will not take it
and the stairs are too narrow.

Perhaps the courtyard will be knee-deep in sunlight and
      pigeons
perhaps there will be snow and children's cries mingling in
      the air
or the asphalt glistening with rain
and the dustbins littering the place as usual.

If in keeping with the custom here I am to go, face open to
      the skies,
on the hearse, a pigeon might drop something on my brow,
      for luck.
Whether a band turns up or no, children will come near me,
children like funerals.

Our kitchen window will stare after me as I go,
the washing in the balcony will wave to see me off.
I have been happier here than you can ever imagine,
friends, I wish you all a long and happy life.

April 1963
Moscow

[TRANSLATED BY FEYYAZ KAYACAN FERGAR]

APPENDIX

Early Poems

1913–1925

'THE WAYS OF GOD'

No caravan ever travels those ways, no bird.
There every night is filled with holy light;
For days they stretch further and further as we walk.
No caravan ever travels those ways, no bird.

For centuries those stony places were deserted.
Today we alone trespass
On their eternal silence.
We have been walking since we first knew God.

DREAM

Last night I saw you in my dream.
We were together by the shore;
We became spirit to the horizons that embraced
The weary high seas as they breathed.

While night, white-speckled and black-veiled,
Was taking a faded day to its breast,
Your eyes were dreamy, I breathed
A secret kiss on your lovely neck.

Hand in hand we laughed at every cheerful star –
I thought happiness would last for ever.
Wanting to be deceived by that alluring girl
Called 'Life' – suddenly I awoke.

Now no night, no sea, no you,
I see no more that radiant place,
Only the rhymes of my wretched poem
Are in my pain-racked heart.

OLD MAN BY THE BRINK OF A STREAM

Looking for consolation for yesterday in the coming day
I walked one evening by the brink of a stream.
The water was dragging through sallow weeds.
The smell of leaves decaying on the banks
Rose from the body of a dying autumn,
A smell from an opened tomb –
I shivered before those dead leaves,
The last bones of the rotting seasons, I said.
A water that surely goes to the cypress groves.
Now I move on, head bent;
Footsteps slow and heavy came behind me,
Turning, I saw an old whitehaired man.
Without a glance he headed straight for the stream.
Looking closely I wondered – what will he do?
He stooped over the rotting leaves on the bank,
His hand scooped up and wiped each leaf,
He embraced them all and held them close –
Then hurled them one by one in the drifting water.
Now his eyes follow them with tears.
The waters grew shadowy, the tired stream flowed.
An autumn night declined in mourning,
Now only an old heap of shadows remained.

16 *October* 1920
Alemdar

WATER WHEEL IN THE KITCHEN GARDEN

Summer evening, I wait in the vines for a wind
Those water-wheels in the garden sadden my heart

The colour of day fades in the puddles
Hoarse creaking as the feeble horse revolves

It groans at every step
The plaintive cry re-echoes in the distance

Its white mane dragged in the wind
Its eyes bound in endless darkness

The poor thing turns and turns, its groans resound . . .
The same path followed, the same spot worn away

And we're the same: our eyes blindfold
We plead with our hearts and pray

Moaning and causing moan, we circle for years
In the same place we start, in the same place we fade away

We say we've progressed but the same path is followed
What we chose is a mansion in this eternal darkness

But finally a day will come when our eyes open
We'll have the last word and be free of the circle.

27 December 1920, 17 *February* 1921
Ümid

FIRST LOOK AT ANATOLIA

We two friends took the road to the hills.
We were so high that Inebolu on the shore
Got smaller and smaller, with its tiny streets,
The minaret just a stroke, the mosque a dot.
The houses in the city joined together
But before us the horizons gradually widened;
And became two open arms embracing the sea.
Wind blew, the ocean waves made roads.

Dry leaves were piled on earth,
Slipping and staggering by them we reached at last
The foot of the final cliff,
The rock at the peak aloof as a haughty head!
If we climbed and looked over we would see
A legendary place we heard of in our childhood,
Beautiful Anatolia would appear.
To engrave it instantly on our hearts
We covered our eyes before the final step.

As we opened our eyes, the Anatolia of our dreams
Now lay before us with her misty valleys;
We saw far down below the road to the stream,
On its right a meadow, pine trees on the left.
The mountain slopes were so near
But spring dropping into the valley could climb no higher.
What a wonderful country! Winter in the mountains,
On the roads autumn, spring in the valley,
And in the golden sunlight, summer's heat.

17 *February* 1921

THE DARK FANATICAL FORCES

For centuries instead of heaven's eternal light,
The gloom of dark fanatical forces
Has pervaded the purest, cleanest hearts
Of this land.

For centuries this dark power,
A wound that bleeds in our souls,
Has growled like a parched wolf
Whenever the country ran towards radiant light.

While the swart hands of this dark force
Encircle our throats,
We, in our hearts, still give this thief
The most sacred place.

But ungrateful are all the Faithful
If they don't kneel and give thanks to God
When those hands that steal youth's sacred light
Are cut off like the hands of a thief.

1921

WANDERLUST

A clear calm night, the horizon hung with stars;
What longing it gave us to run for hours,
Awoke in us the need to be thrown,
To be hurled, beyond space and time.

We wanted the colour of the sky to change a little,
To listen to the nightingale by cool streams,
To bind dear Ayşe's hair with its five plaits,
And weep with the sorrow of inns full of exiles.
We wanted the ocean's briny waters to splash our brows,
To lie in the shade of yellow banana trees,
To taste with our hands that fruit like foam.
We wanted the rose-bodied women's lips to pale
With the heat of our passion
And the years to roll by in succession.
To drink the most perfumed syrups in one gulp,
That seemed to turn us crazy.
To go by places cheerful with light and sound,
To let music tell us of unknown griefs.
We wanted our eyes to be full of people with strong faces,
Who promise the world a new fortune.

A clear calm night, the horizon hung with stars;
What longing it gave us to run for hours,
Awoke in us the need to be thrown,
To be hurled, beyond space and time.

1921

NOTES

Extracts from the Diary of La Gioconda (page 32)

35   *zurna* is a reed instrument like an oboe.

36   *Leylâ and Mejnun* were the famous lovers of an eastern romance and the equivalent of Romeo and Juliet.

The Epic of Sheikh Bedreddin (page 51)

53   *fief*: in the Ottoman feudal system, land granted to the peasant in exchange for military service.

54   *Teshil*: the book that clarified and summarized Bedreddin's beliefs.

56   *Varidât*: the work in which Sheikh Bedreddin set out his utopian beliefs that the world would change after a great revolution in which poverty, injustice and social inequalities would be eliminated. Hikmet saw in Bedreddin's philosophy a paradigm of his own vision for the future, based on the materialist philosophy of Karl Marx.

61   In part 9 Hikmet is answering imaginary critics who may here accuse him of separating mind from heart: he argues that 'A Marxist is not a mechanical man or a ROBOT. He is, with his flesh, blood, nerves and brain and heart, a historical, social and concrete human being.' [Nâzım]

The Turkish Peasant (page 79)

Throughout this remarkable poem Hikmet has incorporated lines from Turkish folk poetry and from songs sung by Turkish soldiers at the time of Gallipoli and the War of Independence.

79   *Nasreddin Hodja*: 'the wise fool', who, with his donkey, figures in fables and comic anecdotes of village life; found also in the works of the Sufis.

79   *Zihni*: a folk poet.

79   *Ferhad, Kerem, Keloğlan*: characters in Turkish fable and romance. Ferhad is Şirin's lover, Kerem is Aslı's lover, and Keloğlan a folk-hero who starts off poor and unknown but wins success through his talents.

79   *Wretched Yunus*: Yunus Emre, the great mediaeval mystic poet of Turkey, who wrote in simple language all could understand.

Poems Written Between 9 and 10 at Night (page 83)

90 *the ballad of Memo*: Memo was a Robin Hood figure who lived in north-east Turkey at the end of the 19th century, robbing the rich to give to the poor.

'I love my country' (page 100)

100 *Bedreddin*: the 15th-century Sheikh who proposed an early form of socialism and was involved in a peasant rebellion against Ottoman feudalism. (See also 'The Epic of Sheikh Bedreddin', p. 50 ff.)

100 *Sinan*: the great 16th-century Turkish architect.

100 *Yunus Emre*: considered by some to be the greatest Turkish poet of all time (d. 1321).

100 *Sakarya*: the battle of 1921, when Greek forces were driven from the mainland at Izmir by Atatürk.

Letters from Çankırı Prison (page 113)

114 *Gazalî*: more likely to be the 16th-century Ottoman poet from Bursa than the early philosopher and mystic (b. 1058).

115 *Keyhüsrev*: Cyrus the Great, the Persian monarch. Nâzım quotes Gazalî as the English poet Shelley quoted Ozymandias, 'Look on my works, ye Mighty, and despair!'

116 *bağlama*: a smaller version of the *saz*, a musical instrument.

Lodos (page 130)

130 *Lodos*: a south-west wind. Turkish proverbs tell that it comes from Hell (*cehennemden gelir*) and that it brings tears, i.e. rain (*Lodosun gözü yaşlı olur*). It has an enervating and sometimes disturbing effect.

Quatrains (page 146)

'Now I've begun a new book called "Rubailer to Piraye". It will consist of about forty quatrains . . . I am trying to do something never done before in western or eastern literature, namely to present Dialectical Materialism in the form of quatrains. I can succeed, I'm sure, with the help of your love; I'll be doing the exact opposite of what Mevlana did with the help of God's love'. [Extract from letter to Piraye from Bursa prison, December 1945]

'Dear Wife,
     The Rubaiyat to Piraye will have four sections: the first will be philosophical, the second social, the third only love quatrains, and

the fourth satirical. There will be 25 quatrains in each section, 100 in all.' [Extract from letter written January 1946]

In Bursa's Fortress Prison (page 159)

159 *Bedreddin*: Nâzım had already written, in 1936, the long poem on the heroic leader of a peasant revolt – 'The Epic of Sheikh Bedreddin', p. 51 ff.

Uludağ (page 162)

162 *the Monk*: Monk Mountain (Keşiş Dağı), Mount Olympus near Bursa (now named Uludağ).

On Living (page 165)

165 *Nasreddin Hodja*: a Turkish folk character; a 'wise fool', hero of innumerable stories. He is always pictured riding back to front on his donkey.

Testament (page 179)

179 *Bey*: the old title used after a man's first name, signifying 'country gentleman', 'sir'. (Now often replaced by Bay which precedes the name.)

179 *forty days*: on the 40th day after the birth a special ceremony for the mother and child was held at the hamam.

The Postman (page 182)

182 *ayran*: a salty drink of yoghourt and water.

The Last Bus (page 198)

'He understood how seriously ill he was, he knew he was going to die. What pain he must have felt when he wrote this poem.' – Müzehher Vâ-Nû

Bees (page 207)

Nâzım's last love-affair was with Vera Tulyakova. She went to take a holiday on the Black Sea with her husband, but Nâzım followed her there. He eventually married her.

Morning Darkness (page 215)

215 *börek*: small filo pastry puffs filled with cheese or other fillings.

Flaxen Hair (page 219)

227 *Jelaleddin Rumi*: the greatest Persian mystical poet (1207–1273), who migrated to Konya in Asia Minor and founded the Mevlevi order of Dervishes.

My Funeral (page 237)

This was one of the last poems Nâzım Hikmet wrote.

INDEX OF TITLES

References in brackets give the volume and page of the Adam Yayınları edition of Nâzım Hikmet's Collected Works. Initials identify the translator; RC/RM indicates a joint translation by Ruth Christie and Richard McKane.

A1   *835 Satır* (835 Lines)
A2   *Benerci Kendini Niçin Öldürdü?* (Why Did Benerjee Kill Himself?)
A3   *Kuvâyi Milliye* (The Epic of the War of Independence)
A4   *Yatar Bursa Kalesinde* (In Bursa's Fortress Prison)
A6   *Yeni Şiirler* (New Poems)
A7   *Son Şiirleri* (Last Poems)
A8   *İlk Şiirler* (Early Poems)

FF   Feyyaz Kayacan Fergar
RC   Ruth Christie
RM   Richard McKane
TH   Talât Sait Halman

Also translated by Ruth Christie
and Richard McKane

Poems of
OKTAY RIFAT

INTRODUCED BY CEVAT ÇEPAN

For half a century, until his death in 1988, Oktay Rifat occupied
a leading position in the vanguard of Turkish poetry. Despite
his popularity and fame he rarely appeared in public, preferring
the private life of an ordinary family man and content to work as
a lawyer while continuing to write.

His extraordinary poetry falls into three periods: the early *Garip
Group* phase of audacious revolt against tradition; then the neo-
surrealist period of avant-garde experimentation; and finally his
mature period of polished formal fusion, when he blended folk
traditions with aesthetic innovation.

Rifat insisted throughout that "Poetry must be read and must be
readable." Striving always for accessibility, he used everyday
language and metaphors drawn from nature to create poetry
rich in feeling and thought. This large and beautifully translated
selection from all phases of Rifat's work demonstrates why his
poetry retains its high place in the affections of Turkish readers.

Born in Trezibond on the Black Sea, Oktay Rifat (1914–1988)
was the son of a Turkish MP. After studying in Paris before the
Second World War he became a lawyer and worked for most of
his life as a legal adviser for Turkish State Railways.

POETRY BOOK SOCIETY RECOMMENDED TRANSLATION